HALIFAX
EXPLOSION

Heroes and Survivors

JOYCE GLASNER

Formac Publishing Company Limited
Halifax

Formac Publishing Company Limited recognizes the support of the Province of Nova Scotia through the Department of Communities, Culture and Heritage – Creative Industries Fund. We are pleased to work in partnership with the Province of Nova Scotia to develop and promote our cultural resources for all Nova Scotians. We acknowledge the support of the Canada Council for the Arts, which last year invested $153 million to bring the arts to Canadians throughout the country. This project has been made possible in part by the Government of Canada.

Cover design: Tyler Cleroux

Library and Archives Canada Cataloguing in Publication

Glasner, Joyce, author
        Halifax explosion : heroes and survivors / Joyce Glasner.

Previously published: Toronto : James Lorimer & Company Ltd, ©2011.
Includes bibliographical references and index.
Issued in print and electronic formats.
ISBN 978-1-4595-0523-0 (softcover).--ISBN 978-1-4595-0524-7 (EPUB)

    1. Halifax Explosion, Halifax, N.S., 1917. I. Title.

FC2346.4.G53 2018   971.6'22503   C2018-900196-8
                                               C2018-900197-6

Formac Publishing Company Limited
5502 Atlantic Street
Halifax, Nova Scotia, Canada
B3H 1G4
www.formac.ca

Printed and bound in Korea.

CONTENTS

PROLOGUE

The Halifax waterfront in the early 20th century prior to the explosion.

As the night express from Saint John to Halifax neared Rockingham on the morning of December 6, 1917, Conductor J. C. Gillespie pulled out his pocket watch to check the time again. The No. 10, as it was officially known, was now running about ten minutes late. Since it was Gillespie's job to keep everything aboard running smoothly, he fretted about being so far behind schedule. Just as he slipped his watch back into his pocket, something slammed into the train with what felt like the force of a torpedo. Shrieks and gasps filled the air as each of the windows shattered in unison. Gillespie staggered and almost landed in the aisle as the cars tipped up, balancing precariously on one rail. They hung there, suspended at a crazy angle, for a second or two before dropping back to the tracks with a resounding crash.

Once he'd regained his footing, Gillespie hurried through the cars, checking on the passengers. Everyone was shaken by the incident, but fortunately no one was injured. In the locomotive, however, Gillespie found the engineer in bad shape. The man had been hurled against the boiler head and been badly burned. But he insisted on remaining at the controls until they reached Halifax.

The cause of the crash was a mystery. The line was clear, and as far as they could determine the train hadn't struck anything. The only plausible explanation was that a cataclysmic concussion had occurred somewhere down the line. Although battered, the train was still operational, so they proceeded cautiously towards the city. One of the passengers on board that morning was Colonel Earle Caleb Phinney, who had recently returned from France. As they crept past Africville, the African-Canadian community on the shore of the Bedford Basin, Phinney studied the ominous cloud of smoke curling high above Halifax's North End. There was only one thing that could have caused a cloud like that — a massive explosion. Was it possible that the long-anticipated German attack on Halifax had finally begun?

Chapter 1
COLLISION COURSE

In Halifax Harbour, Captain Horatio Brannen and his crew aboard the SS *Stella Maris* were preparing to haul two scows of ashes from the Dockyard into the Bedford Basin. It was a clear, crisp morning, and the crew cursed and blew on numb fingers as they worked to secure the lines to the scows. Brannen had been in the salvage business for almost two decades. He'd started out working in the fishing industry as a boy, and by the time he was twenty-eight he'd achieved the rank of captain. Since then, he'd conducted numerous daring salvage and rescue operations that had earned him a reputation for being calm and courageous in the face of danger. Six months earlier, he'd had a narrow escape when his own vessel, *Deliverance,* was struck by another ship while sweeping for mines off Portuguese Cove. Determined to save his vessel, Brannen had remained on board until the very last moment and almost ended up going down with his ship. In comparison, towing the scows was a simple job, and Brannen didn't anticipate any problems that morning.

Just as the *Stella Maris* got underway, however, Brannen spied a ship coming through the Narrows and heading

The SS Stella Maris, *pictured in Halifax Harbour only months prior to the explosion.*

straight towards them. With the unwieldy scows in tow, it would be impossible to reach the opposite side of the channel in time to avoid a collision. He swung the tug back towards the Dockyard, reaching it just in the nick of time. As the steamer sailed past, he noted the name *Imo* on the bow and the words "Belgian Relief" in large, red letters on its hull.

The *Imo*, a 5,041-ton Norwegian tramp steamer, had been chartered by the Belgian Relief Commission to transport supplies from North America to the war-torn nation of Belgium. The tramp steamer should have been halfway down the eastern seaboard by then, but had spent the previous day anchored in the Bedford Basin awaiting a coal shipment. By the time the coal arrived and was transferred aboard, the anti-submarine net — a network of mines that was stretched across the harbour each evening at dusk — was already in place. As a result, they were forced to spend an extra night in port. The delay irritated Captain Hakkon From, who was anxious to proceed to New York, where they were to pick up a load of grain before heading across the Atlantic. From urged pilot William Hayes to speed up their passage through the harbour. Hays complied. He pushed the steamer two knots over the harbour's speed limit, despite the fact that the helm was sluggish and harbour traffic heavy.

Halifax sits on a large peninsula that juts out into the harbour — a deep, spacious, ice-free body of water that narrows to a bottleneck between Halifax and Dartmouth and then broadens out into the Bedford Basin at the northern end of the peninsula. The city's proximity to the North Atlantic shipping routes, as well the harbour's size and shape, made Halifax one of the most valuable seaports in the British Empire at that time. By 1917, the harbour teemed with allied cruisers, freighters, and merchant ships. And more

Captain Horatio Brannen of the SS *Stella Maris.*

often than not, a smattering of camouflaged and zebra-striped vessels awaiting convoy swung at anchor in the Bedford Basin. There were forty-five vessels in the harbour that morning, and every pier swarmed with sailors and stevedores loading and unloading shipments of lumber, food, horses and equipment.

As the *Imo* sped through the Narrows, it met an American freighter, which had been the first vessel admitted into the harbour when the boom opened at dawn. The freighter was too far into the *Imo*'s water to correct its course in time for the vessels to pass one another in the conventional port-to-port manner. So the skipper of the American ship signalled that he was maintaining course to the left. The *Imo* acknowledged the signal, and the ships steamed past one another without incident. The *Imo* then continued along on the same course.

The battered Imo, *beached on the Dartmouth shore.*

After witnessing this incident, Captain Brannen was relieved he'd decided to swing the *Stella Maris* back towards the Halifax shore. Standing next to him on the bridge was his son and first mate, Walter Brannen, and crewmember William Knickerson. As they watched the *Imo* barrel through the busy harbour, all three had a bad feeling about its relentless pace. But Brannen had a job to do. He pushed his concerns aside and ordered the crew back to work. He swung the tug around and was once again about to set out for the Bedford Basin when a grey freighter appeared on the horizon.

* * *

It was a twist of fate that brought the *Mont-Blanc* to Halifax that morning. The 3,121-ton freighter should have been halfway to Bordeaux by that time. The *Mont-Blanc* was owned and operated by Compagnie Générale Transatlantique, a French shipping firm. Currently, however, she was under French

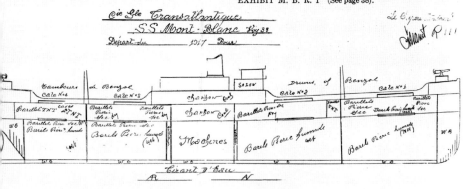

A layout of Mont-Blanc's *explosive cargo bound for France.*

naval orders. At the helm of the battered eighteen-year-old freighter was Captain Aimé Le Médec, a short, dark-haired thirty-eight-year-old who had served with the company for just over a decade.

The *Mont-Blanc* had sailed from Bordeaux in November with orders to proceed to Gravesend Bay, New York, where it would pick up cargo and return to France.

Prior to their arrival in New York, Le Médec hadn't been informed about the nature of the cargo they were to transport across the Atlantic. So it came as a shock when the stevedores began loading the hold with 2,300 tons of picric acid, 200 tons of TNT, 10 tons of gun cotton, and 35 tons of benzol. Although he'd had no previous experience with explosives, Le Médec knew this was enough lethal material to blow the *Mont-Blanc* — and anything within range — to smithereens.

The company had taken precautions to ensure the volatile cargo was safely stowed in the hold. And the drums of highly flammable benzol were stored on deck, as far from the other materials as possible. Nevertheless, the thought of sailing across the Atlantic on what was essentially a floating bomb was unsettling.

Just when Le Médec thought things couldn't get much worse, he was informed that the convoy in which they were scheduled to sail back to Bordeaux had refused to take them along. Making the crossing alone was unthinkable at that time. The Atlantic was infested with German subs lying in wait

Harbour pilot Francis Mackey.

for allied vessels. The British Navy had lost hundreds of ships in battles with German U-boats over the past few months. As a result, naval and merchant vessels had begun travelling in packs. Speed was of the utmost importance to every convoy. But with the load she was carrying, the *Mont-Blanc* could barely manage seven knots for any distance. This made it a liability that the convoy wasn't prepared to deal with. So rather than heading directly back to Bordeaux with his cargo, Le Médec was forced to sail up the coast to Halifax. There, he was told, they might hook up with a larger convoy — one accompanied by a cruiser for added protection.

* * *

When the *Mont-Blanc* arrived at the examination anchorage at the mouth of Halifax Harbour the previous evening, harbour pilot Francis Mackey came aboard. Mackey, a stocky forty-five-year-old with a quarter of a century of experience under his belt, would be guiding the freighter into the harbour. Mackey informed Le Médec that the anti-submarine net was already in place, which meant they'd have to spend the night outside the protective shelter of the harbour. After the stressful five-day voyage from New York, Le Médec was anxious to get into the harbour as soon as possible. He asked Mackey to stay on board that night, so they could get underway at first light.

At 7:30 the next morning, the *Mont-Blanc* was cleared to enter the harbour. Le Médec breathed a sigh of relief as they crept towards the outer boom. Mackey's knowledge of the harbour was impressive. Every inlet, jut of shoreline, shoal, and shallow was etched in his memory. Le Médec found the pilot's confidence and familiarity with the harbour reassuring. As they slipped through the outer boom, he began to feel optimistic for the first time since leaving New York. They'd made it this far without incident. Maybe, just maybe, they'd find a convoy here that would agree to escort them home.

* * *

As the *Mont-Blanc* sailed into the harbour that morning, the city was just beginning to stir. War had transformed Halifax from a sedate backwater to a thriving metropolis of 50,000, crowded with servicemen on their way to or from the front. In addition to the influx of soldiers and sailors, hordes of enterprising individuals, including businessmen, bootleggers, and prostitutes, had also flocked to the city hoping to profit from the wartime boom. Prohibition had been in effect for a year, but booze flowed freely in the numerous bootleg joints, known as blind pigs. The parties in these establishments went on till the wee hours of the morning. And more often than not, inebriated patrons were just stumbling home as cart-drivers, hawking everything from coal to dairy products, prepared for their morning rounds.

In this city divided by class and race, Citadel Hill marked the line between north and south, rich and poor. In the South End, elegant Victorian mansions lined the shaded avenues from Spring Garden Road to Point Pleasant Park. At the opposite end of the peninsula was the ramshackle African-Canadian community of Africville. Between these polar opposites was the working-class community of Richmond. Those who grew up in Richmond tended to remain there, usually working in the same factories their parents and grandparents had helped

A meeting of the Halifax Rowing Club, with the Acadia Sugar Refinery in the background.

build. Dominion Textiles, the Acadia Sugar Refinery, Hillis & Sons Iron Foundry, and Richmond Printing Company dominated the landscape and the lives of just about everyone in the area. In this closely knit community, everyone knew their neighbours, and large extended families lived cheek by jowl, often all under one roof.

The Intercolonial Railway Station, commonly known as North Street Station, was a central landmark in the North End. The brick building featured a domed central tower, round-top windows, and a canopy of iron and glass that soared above the platforms. The cavernous station was bustling that morning as the Suburban arrived in a cacophony of shrieking brakes and clanking wheels.

Evelyn Fox stepped off the train and slung her book-bag over her shoulder. As the fifteen-year-old and her father threaded their way through the crowded station, she drank in every detail. Arthur Fox had recently been appointed principal of the Alexandra School in Halifax, which meant moving the family from the small coastal community of Clark's Harbour to the suburb of Bedford. Evelyn was still enthralled by the hustle and bustle of city life. As she later

14

wrote, "I savoured every raucous note, every mote of air pollution." Although Evelyn's younger sister and brothers went to school in Bedford, she had to travel to the city to attend the Halifax County Academy, which sat at the foot of Citadel Hill. Most mornings she travelled aboard the 8:20 milk train. But that morning she happened to be up earlier than usual and decided to accompany her father on the 7:30 Suburban.

Evelyn, who would later become a well-known local author, was the third of seven children. Her two older brothers, Ashford and Douglas, had both enlisted with the Canadian Military as soon as they were of age. Ashford was currently serving in France, and Douglas was a recruit in training at the Brunswick Street Barracks. Having a brother in France, Evelyn was particularly sympathetic to the multitude of sailors and soldiers in the city, especially those she'd see in the station "pleading for a smile and a wave, even from strangers, before they marched to the pier for embarkation and the battlefields."

Richmond Railyards prior to the explosion.

Nova Scotia had one of the highest rates of enlistment in the country during World War I. The Nova Scotia Highlanders, in particular, attracted enough recruits to form not one, but *four* battalions. By 1917, so many Haligonians were serving overseas that there were few able-bodied men left in the city. Indeed, there was hardly a family in the city that wasn't affected one way or another by the war.

Vincent Coleman.

After leaving the station, Evelyn and her father, each lost in thought, walked in companionable silence up North Street to Brunswick, where they parted ways. Had she known how changed the city would be after that morning, Evelyn would have paid more attention to the sights and sounds along the way. "My mind might have registered, and my memory retained, more precise details," she later wrote.

* * *

Over on Russell Street, Vincent Coleman stepped outside and took a deep breath. The pleasantly crisp air was tinged with a hint of briny harbour scent, and a light frost dusted the rooftops. As he set out for his office in the railway yard, his thoughts turned to the upcoming union meeting and the badly needed wage increase the union was pushing for. With Christmas only a few weeks away, the extra money would certainly come in handy. The forty-three-year-old was a train dispatcher with the Canadian Government Railway. Like his father and older brother Chris, Vincent was a dyed-in-the-wool railway man. His father, Daniel, had worked for the CGR most of his life, and the old man had been filled with pride when his two boys had decided to follow in his footsteps, Chris becoming an engineer and Vincent a dispatcher. Vincent's dedication to the company was undeniable. In fact, a few months earlier he'd been hailed as a local hero after he'd leaped aboard a

Frances Coleman.

runaway engine and brought it to a halt in time to prevent a collision with another train. His co-worker, William Lovett, still ribbed him about that episode.

After her husband left for work, Frances Coleman stirred the porridge and called Eleanor, Gerald, and Nita down to breakfast. Vincent and Frances had been married for fifteen years. In that time, they'd had their ups and downs, but the past year had been particularly difficult. Their two boys, Gerald and Cyril, had contracted diphtheria the previous year. This highly contagious upper-respiratory tract infection was a leading cause of death for children at the time, and was known as "the strangling angel of children." During their illness, the boys were quarantined in one room of the house, and no one but Frances was allowed near them. After leaving the quarantined area, she changed her clothes and washed up thoroughly before going near the rest of the family. The Colemans' youngest, Babe, was just five months old, and Frances was terrified that she might contract the disease. Gerald, the oldest boy, survived the illness. But eight-year-old Cyril did not. Losing their youngest son was devastating. It was the type of blow that might have torn the family apart, but the couple's commitment to each other and their children pulled them through.

After Cyril's death, the family moved into the house on Russell Street. They'd been saving for their own house for years. Moving to the new place had been a blessing for the family, an opportunity to leave the bad times behind and make a fresh start.

That morning, seven-year-old Eleanor would be the only one going to school. Her older sister Nita had come down with strep throat and was staying home with Frances and the baby, while Gerald was scheduled to serve as an altar boy at morning mass at St. Joseph's Church. Until recently, the boys and girls of St. Joseph's parish attended separate schools. But the boys' school had burned down the previous year. So until the new school was finished, boys and girls shared the same space, the girls attending classes in the morning and the boys in the afternoon.

* * *

As the *Mont-Blanc* neared the Narrows, Captain Le Médec and Francis Mackey noticed a tramp steamer, well into their side of the channel, heading straight towards them. Le Médec ordered his first mate to give one short whistle blast to indicate he was altering course to starboard. Astonishingly, the *Imo* responded with two blasts, signalling its intention to alter its course to port. This shift in direction would put the *Imo* even further into the French freighter's water. As the two ships attempted to manoeuvre around one another, a flurry of whistle blasts rang out across the harbour.

Aboard the *Stella Maris*, Captain Brannen, Walter Brannen, and William Knickerson watched in disbelief as the *Imo* bore

The Mont-Blanc *and* Imo, *on fire and wedged together in the harbour following the collision.*

down on the French freighter. Something was terribly amiss. Unless one of the vessels changed course immediately, a collision appeared inevitable. Just then, the *Mont-Blanc*'s bow swung hard to port. "They're going to collide!" Knickerson shouted. A few seconds later, the *Imo*'s bow sliced into the *Mont-Blanc*'s starboard bow.

For Captain Aimé Le Médec, the moment of impact must have seemed like a waking nightmare. Although it had missed the hold containing the explosives, the Norwegian ship's bow had cut a three-metre gash in the *Mont-Blanc*'s starboard bow. Le Médec quickly pulled himself together and ordered the engines reversed. Captain From did the same. As the *Imo*'s bow withdrew from the slash, the grinding sound of metal on metal filled the air, and a spray of sparks showered across the *Mont-Blanc*'s deck. The impact of the collision had

An impression of the Mont-Blanc *on fire by artist Austin Dwyer, 2017.*

snapped the lashings holding the barrels of benzol in place, and they tumbled across the deck and began to leak. The benzol proved to be a perfect accelerant. Once the sparks hit the fuel, it was only a matter of minutes before the *Mont-Blanc*'s deck was engulfed in flames. Clouds of black smoke billowed higher and higher as the fire intensified, fed by the exploding drums of fuel.

Le Médec struggled to remain calm and come up with a viable method of fighting the blaze. Sinking the ship before it blew would have been the best course of action. Time, however, was a critical factor. A dense layer of rust welded the bolts of the seacock to the inlet pipe. Le Médec knew that by the time they managed to remove the rusted bolts, open the valve, and flood the compartments, the powder keg they were standing on would surely have blown to pieces, killing everyone aboard.

While their captain mulled over the situation, the crew, fearing for their lives, had already lowered the two lifeboats into the water. The second Le Médec gave the order to abandon ship, they scurried down ladders and ropes, anxious to get as far from the vessel as they could before she blew.

As soon as First Officer Jean Glotin was sure all hands were safely in the boats, he reported to Le Médec.

"It is time for us to go as well, Captain," he said.

Le Médec, however, had no intention of abandoning ship. It was a captain's duty, he believed, to go down with his vessel. But there was no time to argue the point. Glotin grabbed Le Médec and forced him down the ladder into the waiting boat.

The surviving crew members of the Mont-Blanc *after the explosion.*

21

Chapter 2
THE RED FLAG

After her husband, Jack, left for work at the Dockyard, Catherine James cleared the table and prepared to wash up. As she placed a pot of water on the stove to heat, she glanced out the window and noticed a thick black cloud of smoke hanging above the harbour.

"It must be a ship on fire," she thought. "I hope Jack is alright."

Catherine and John (Jack) James had been married for seventeen years. The couple, originally from Newfoundland, had moved to Sydney, Nova Scotia the year they were married. After he'd completed a blacksmithing apprenticeship, Jack had accepted the job at the Dockyard, and the couple moved to Halifax. Having been raised in a small outport, Catherine found the big city intimidating. She was a shy, uneducated woman. Since moving to the area, she'd made few friends and had become totally dependent on her husband.

The window was too high for Catherine to see much more than the sky, so she pulled a chair over and climbed up for a better look. Still unable to see the exact source of the fire, she stepped down and went back to the sink to get on with her chores.

* * *

The burning ship in the harbour created a buzz throughout the city. The multicoloured flames shooting up to the top of the massive cloud of black smoke caught everyone's attention. Stevedores and sailors dropped what they were doing and gathered in throngs along the wharves to watch the action. Factory workers, merchants, schoolchildren, and housewives rushed to windows, mesmerized by the sight of the blazing freighter as it drifted steadily toward Pier 6.

In the Duggan household on Hanover Street — just a stone's throw from the Dockyard — twenty-year-old Charles Jr. was standing at a window overlooking the Narrows when the collision occurred. As the French freighter burst into flames, he called his wife and parents over to get a look at the fire.

Charles had followed in his father's footsteps and become a ferry pilot. He and his father operated the North ferry,

The Halifax Public Gardens as they exist today.

Halifax's waterfront, abuzz with activity months prior to the explosion.

which plied the waters between the Dockyard and the French cable wharf at Tufts Cove. Fearing there may be men in danger aboard the freighter, Charles decided to go see if he could be of assistance.

"I won't be long," he promised his wife, Rita, before heading out the door.

As he piloted his vessel away from the dock, he noticed the crew of the blazing freighter begin to spill over the side like rats into the waiting lifeboats. Worried that there might still be crew aboard, Charles continued moving toward the vessel. Once he was close enough to feel the heat of the fire on his face, he cut the engine.

* * *

On board the HMCS *Niobe*, Fred Longland hurried up to the forecastle deck. Longland, an officer with the Royal Canadian Navy, had just arrived in Halifax that morning and reported for duty. The *Niobe* was the Royal Canadian Navy's first vessel, purchased second-hand from the British Navy. The shopworn cruiser had seen better days and was now permanently moored at the Dockyard, where she served as a training and depot vessel. Word that the *Niobe* was dispatching a crew in the steam pinnace to battle the blaze had spread rapidly. Before long, the forecastle deck was crowded with curious sailors jostling for a view of the action.

The HMCS Niobe *in drydock in Halifax.*

In the meantime, Captain Brannen had once again ordered the *Stella Maris* back to the Dockyard to drop off the scows before heading over to the burning vessel to offer assistance. As the tug approached the *Mont-Blanc*, Brannen ordered his first mate to break out the hose and prepare to fight the blaze.

Among the vessels in the harbour that morning was the British cruiser HMS *Highflyer*. Captain Garnett had witnessed the collision and was concerned about the fire. Like most others in the harbour that day, he was unaware of the deadly cargo in the *Mont-Blanc's* hold. Nevertheless, a burning ship in such close proximity was a hazard no matter what its cargo — particularly since many vessels in the vicinity had munitions on board. After a brief consultation with his first officer,

The HMS Highflyer.

Commander Tom Triggs, they decided to send a crew over in *Highflyer's* whaler to assess the situation. Triggs volunteered to command the expedition.

A red flag is the international symbol to indicate a ship has explosives on board. The *Mont-Blanc,* however, had not hoisted the red flag before entering the harbour that morning. At the time, enemy spies were thought to be everywhere. With this in mind, Le Médec felt it would be safer not to reveal the nature of his cargo. If word got out that they were carrying explosives, the *Mont-Blanc* would become a sitting duck. As a result, few in the city were aware of the immense threat the burning ship posed.

One of those privy to this information was Commander James Murray, Transport Officer Liaison between the Port Convoy Office and the merchant ships in port. When the collision occurred, Murray was returning from the Bedford Basin aboard the tug *Hilford.* When the tug entered the Narrows, the commander spied the burning vessel. He immediately ordered the helmsman to dock at Pier 9, hoping to reach his office and send out a general alarm before it was too late. As Murray rushed to his office, he ran into a sailor who was sauntering down the street. He ordered the man to spread a warning that the burning ship was loaded with munitions and about to blow.

The *Mont-Blanc* was now perilously close to Pier 6. The railway yardmaster's building, where dispatcher Vincent Coleman and chief clerk William Lovett worked, sat less than 200 metres from the pier. As the burning ship drifted ever closer, the two men kept a close watch on it. The fire posed a serious threat to the yardmaster's building, as well as the dozens of freight cars standing in the yards. When the ship slammed into the jetty, they became alarmed. Within minutes, fire spilled from the deck onto the pier, igniting the wooden pilings and nearby sheds.

By this time, quite a crowd had gathered outside Upham's General Store on Barrington Street. Upham's overlooked the Narrows and offered a perfect view of the spectacle. Everyone was enjoying this unexpected diversion from the regular weekday morning routine. Many speculated on what could be causing the flames to shoot sporadically to the top of the black column of smoke. Others questioned how they'd ever manage to extinguish the fire. When he saw that the burning ship was drifting dangerously close to Pier 6, the store's owner, Constant Upham, rushed to the nearby fire alarm box to alert the fire department. Before long, the clanging of fire bells echoed across the city as the department's brand new motorized pumper, "Patricia," raced to the scene.

The *Stella Maris* was now positioned alongside the blazing *Mont-Blanc*. Captain Brannen and his crew were valiantly attempting to extinguish the raging inferno when Commander Triggs and his crew from the *Highflyer* pulled alongside. Triggs boarded the *Stella Maris* to discuss the situation with Brannen. The best course of action, they decided, would be to attach a line to the *Mont-Blanc* and tow her away from the pier. Out in mid-channel, they reasoned, she would pose less of a threat. This strategy would also allow other tugs to get close enough to help extinguish the fire. At this point, *Niobe*'s steam pinnace — under the command of Acting Bosun Albert Mattison

Jerry Lonecloud.

— had arrived to offer assistance. Confident that Brannen and Mattison could handle the situation, Triggs set off to assess the situation aboard the *Imo*. After the crushing impact, the Norwegian steamer had drifted into mid-channel, where it now lay motionless.

* * *

At Turtle Grove, the small Mi'kmaq settlement on the Dartmouth shore, fifteen-year-old Hannah Lonecloud stood on the beach gazing at the burning vessel. Hannah had never seen anything like it, and she wished her father was there to witness this wondrous sight. Her father, Jerry Lonecloud, was a well known showman, medicine man, and advocate for the Mi'kmaq people. He had travelled extensively throughout North America, and was at one time a performer with Buffalo Bill Cody's Wild West Show. He would certainly have been able to explain what made the multicoloured flames lick the sky like that. But that morning, Jerry was away in Kentville on business. Hannah's mother, Elizabeth, was also away at the time, leaving the fifteen-year-old in the care of her older sister, Rosie.

A few kilometres from Turtle Grove, the fire had also attracted the attention of the residents of Tufts Cove. Aggie Marsh watched the action in the harbour from her front yard.

When she saw the crew of the blazing vessel scurrying over the side and into the boats, she picked up her three-week-old baby and hurried down to join her neighbours on the shore. Everyone was astonished when the boats began pulling toward them, rather than heading for the Halifax shore. The minute the boats reached the shore, most of the sailors clambered out and sprinted off into the woods. But a few paused and shouted *"Courir! Courir!"* as they gestured wildly toward the burning ship and then the woods. The spectators, unable to understand French, just stared at them. The whole thing seemed almost comical until one of the foreigners snatched the baby from Aggie's arms and darted into the woods. In a panic, Aggie, her neighbours, and the rest of the crew followed close on his heels.

* * *

An illustration of Turtle Grove, the Mi'Kmaq settlement in Tufts Cove.

Two young sailors sporting Royal Canadian Navy uniforms.

While those onshore gazed in awe at the fire, Charles Duggan sat in his boat a few hundred metres from the *Mont-Blanc*, keeping a close eye on it. Although he'd seen the men abandon ship, he wanted to be sure there were no stragglers on board before heading back to shore. When he spied the *Stella Maris* and the whaler from the British cruiser pull alongside, he figured the navy had the situation under control and he wouldn't be needed. He started up the launch and was just swinging around to head home when a deep rumbling sound sent a chill down his spine. He turned to see the barrels of benzol on the *Mont-Blanc*'s deck hurtling high into the air and bursting into flames with a roar. Fearful of what would happen next, he opened up the throttle and sped toward the Dartmouth shore.

A quiet morning on Barrington Street before the explosion.

* * *

In the railway yardmaster's office, Vincent Coleman and William Lovett were still debating whether or not they should clear out. The argument was heating up when the sailor sent by Commander Murray stuck his head in the door.

"That ship's loaded with explosives and about to blow!" he shouted.

Without another word, Vincent and William dropped everything and bolted out the door and across the tracks toward Barrington Street. Before long, however, William sensed that the dispatcher was no longer behind him. He turned to see his friend dashing back toward the office.

"What the hell are you doing, Vincent?" he hollered.

"No. 10 is due in at any minute," Vincent yelled over his shoulder. "I've got to warn Rockingham to hold it up."

Chapter 3
LIKE ALL THUNDERS ROLLED INTO ONE

The apocalyptic blast ripped through the city with a force and fury beyond imagination. At approximately 9:05 a.m., 3,121 tons of iron and steel exploded into millions of fragments, flying for miles in all directions. Houses swayed, straightened up, and then collapsed, like houses made of cards. Factories toppled and churches crumbled. Ships, trains, and automobiles were hurled about like toys. Roads were obliterated and railway tracks were torn from the earth. Trees and telephone poles snapped like matchsticks. A torrent of debris was scattered everywhere. The blast shattered every window for miles around, and stilettos of glass flew through the air, ripping through flesh and lodging in eyeballs. Gas lines ruptured, and fire from hundreds of stoves spilled out onto the heaps of kindling created by the blast. Greasy black rain fell from the sky, and shrapnel pelted down over the ruins for several minutes. The harbour became a seething cauldron. Its floor split open,

The resulting mushroom cloud from the explosion, likely taken from the Bedford Basin only moments after the blast.

propelling boulders up from the deep. The force of the blast created a tidal wave, which swamped the shore. Small ships were swallowed and spat back out, and large vessels were ripped from their moorings and flung onto shore.

When it was all over, at least 1,900 people were dead, 9,000 were injured, and hundreds were permanently blinded. Hundreds of victims were buried beneath the wreckage, and fires raged throughout the area. The communities of Richmond, Tufts Cove, and Turtle Grove were laid waste, and Halifax

The Halifax City Hall clock has remained stuck at 9:05 since the day of the explosion.

and Dartmouth were devastated. Electricity, gas, telephone, and telegraph lines were all severed, leaving the city completely crippled.

The situation in the harbour was desperate. Thick black smoke hung over the water, ravaged ships drifted helplessly on the currents, and bodies and debris of every kind littered the shore. Of the forty-five vessels in the harbour, almost all sustained serious damage and extensive casualties. The *Stella Maris*, being closest to the *Mont-Blanc*, had taken the full force of the blast. Amazingly, the little tug was not demolished but blown downstream, where it came to rest near the dry dock. It was stripped of its smokestack and spars, but still intact. Five crewmembers survived, including William Knickerson and Walter Brannen, who had been driven below deck by the blast. But Captain Horatio Brannen and eighteen of his crew died instantly.

Commander Tom Triggs was also killed in the blast. Miraculously, however, a few of his crew in *Highflyer*'s whaler survived. The *Imo* was hurled onto the Dartmouth shore and her superstructure demolished. And Captain Hakkon From and Pilot William Hayes were both killed.

Aboard the *Niobe*, Fred Longland scrambled for cover as a hail of boiler tubes, rivets, and jagged steel plates hammered the deck. The crew dove into ventilator shafts and beneath lifeboats in an effort to dodge the deadly storm of flying debris. When the tidal wave hit, the massive vessel was ripped from its moorings and heaved high into the air before being slammed back to the surface. When it was all over, the main deck was a disaster. All four of the ship's funnels were

Piers 7, 8, and 9 were completely obliterated by the blast.

demolished and its superstructure destroyed. In all, nineteen men, including Albert Mattison and the crew of the steam pinnace, were killed. Dozens were critically wounded.

The *Hilford*, which was at Pier 9, was blown out of the water and severely damaged. The *Curaca*, which had been unloading horses at Pier 8, was blown right across the harbour and sank at Tufts Cove. The *Calonne*, which had been loading horses at Pier 9, was ravaged and thirty-six of her crew killed, while the British vessel *Picton*, which had a load of munitions on board, was badly damaged and set ablaze.

In addition, the Dockyard, Naval College, and several wharves were pulverized. For the first time in its long history, Halifax Harbour, one of the busiest, most vital ports in the British Empire, was paralyzed.

* * *

When Charles Duggan came to, he was onshore. He had no idea how long he had been unconscious, where he was, or how he got there. The last thing he remembered was watching

35

The few ships that remained afloat after the explosion drifted aimlessly in the harbour.

the huge cloud of smoke rising from the burning ship as he sat in his launch, a few hundred metres away. As he later told a reporter from the *Daily Echo,* the blazing ship "seemed to settle in the water. A lurid yellowish-green spurt of flame rose toward the heaven and drove ahead of it a cloud of smoke, which must have risen 200 feet in the air." Then came the most appalling crash he had ever heard. His launch seemed to be snatched from beneath his feet "as if some supernatural power had stolen her." He was plunged into the icy harbour and "engulfed in a swirling, roaring mass of water," which drove him to the bottom like a stone. After what seemed like an eternity, he surfaced — only to be caught up in a second raging wave…

Charles sat up and looked around. He felt dizzy and disoriented. But after a few moments he realized he was on the Dartmouth shore, near the French cable wharf — almost directly across the harbour from his home. Up ahead, he saw what appeared to be the remains of his eleven-metre boat cast ashore. Another, much larger vessel was grounded a little further down. It was tipped at an odd angle and looked badly damaged. In the distance, he heard screams and cries for help.

As he struggled to his feet and glanced around, Charles was sickened by what he saw. The landscape had been transformed into a charred and barren wilderness. Mingled among the piles of debris littering the beach were blackened, mangled corpses and dismembered body parts. A dense layer of smoke hung over the water and black plumes spiralled upwards here and there. Damaged vessels, ripped from their moorings, drifted among the debris floating on the surface.

Suddenly, the memory of his family came to him, of Rita and their young son Warren waving goodbye as he left the house earlier. He had to get home. In a panic, he began staggering down the beach. Charles eventually came upon a general store, which was in flames. In his dazed condition, however, the fact that the store was on fire didn't really register. He stepped through the door and immediately passed

The Richmond Railyards, bustling with activity only hours earlier, were all but erased from the landscape.

The Hour of Horror in Devastated Richmond, *sketched in 1918 by Arthur Lismer, who was in Halifax on the day of the explosion.*

out again. When he came to some time later, he was choking on the dense smoke that filled the store. He crawled out the door and tried to focus on getting to the south ferry landing.

When Charles finally made it to the landing, he was amazed to find that the ferries were still operating. He boarded the first one that docked, intent on getting home. During the crossing, he overheard the other passengers discussing the explosion and the devastation in the North End. He prayed that the rumours about Richmond being nothing but a funeral pyre were exaggerated.

* * *

While Charles Duggan was trying to orient himself, a few kilometres down shore Captain Aimé Le Médec pulled himself to his feet and looked around in disbelief. There wasn't a tree left standing anywhere in the vicinity. Aggie Marsh's baby was wailing loudly. Everyone else was silent. Le Médec's hands trembled as he pulled out his cigarettes and jammed one into his mouth. It was only when he began groping around in his pockets for a match that he remembered they had been banned aboard ship. First Officer Jean Glotin was busy trying to round up the crew for a roll call. But several of the frightened men had disappeared into the charred wilderness. After checking on the rest, Glotin reported that although several crewmembers had sustained minor injuries, only one man was critically wounded and in urgent need of medical attention.

* * *

On Barrington Street, Ada Moore had just kissed her husband, Charles, and their four older children goodbye and got them out the door that morning when the sight of the blazing vessel in the harbour caught her attention. The baby, one-month-old Catherine, was sleeping peacefully in her carriage in the dining room, but four-year-old Jack and the seventeen-month-old twins were restless. Hoping to distract them for a while, Ada set the twins in a chair at one window and Jack at another to watch the spectacle. She was standing in the open doorway when the postman, Mr. Spruce, came along. After he'd handed Ada her mail, they chatted about the fire for a few minutes before the postman turned to go. He hadn't taken two steps before the vessel exploded.

* * *

Mr. Spruce was killed instantly, and Ada was knocked unconscious. Several minutes later, the tidal wave swept over her and she came to, sputtering and coughing. When she tried to move, she discovered that she was out in the street, pinned beneath two beams. After a struggle, she managed to free herself and got to her feet. She was knee-deep in icy water and wearing nothing but her undergarments. The house had collapsed and the children were buried beneath the wreckage, which had caught fire. In a panic, Ada grabbed the first man to come along and begged him to help rescue the children. The two tried again and again to get to them, but the smoke and searing heat of the flames prevented them from reaching Ada's babies.

By the time it became apparent that there was no use in trying to reach the children anymore, Ada was traumatized. Although she was almost paralyzed with grief, she knew she had to find her four older children, who attended Richmond School. As she stumbled up Roome Street in a daze, a woman came out and wrapped a blanket around her shoulders. Only then did she become vaguely aware of the fact that she wasn't wearing anything but her drenched undergarments.

Richmond School had been ravaged in the explosion, and what remained standing was ablaze. Ada searched the entire area but found no trace of the children. She wandered over the hill to Lady Hammond Road, where another good Samaritan took pity on the obviously distraught thirty-five-year-old and gave her a knitted coat. Eventually, Ada found herself in the woods off Lady Hammond Road, where she met up with a group of people trying to stay warm around a fire.

A devastated Richmond School in the days following the explosion.

Glass shrapnel from shattered windows all across the city left many blinded.

* * *

Catherine James had just returned to the sink to begin washing the breakfast dishes when the explosion occurred. She was knocked face down on the floor and blacked out as the house collapsed on top of her. When she came to, she was buried in timbers and plaster. She screamed for help, but no one came. She lay there for a while feeling dazed and helpless. Then she caught a whiff of smoke and remembered stoking the fire and placing the pot of water on the stove to heat. Panic-stricken, Catherine pushed at the timbers with all her strength, but they barely budged. When she tried wriggling out from under them, nails and splinters ripped her flesh. She was ready to give up, but the thought of being roasted alive forced her to keep trying. Finally, she managed to move the timbers enough to be able to squirm out from under them.

Catherine crawled from the wreckage minutes before the whole building went up in flames. As she stood up and looked around, she was stunned by what she encountered. The

41

Artist Judy Csukly's abstract painting evokes the devastation of Richmond in the wake of the explosion.

entire hillside was on fire, and about the only structure left standing in the vicinity was the blazing remains of Richmond School on the brow of the hill.

She began to shiver violently and realized she was wearing nothing but a thin cotton housedress. Something wet trickled down her face. When she reached up and touched her head, she discovered it was bleeding. Uncertain of what to do next, Catherine sat down near the burning house and waited for Jack to come home.

Some time later, a soldier came along and found the slender, dark-haired woman huddled next to the smouldering remains of her home. When he tried to convince her to leave the ruins, she refused, saying that she was waiting for her husband, who would surely be home anytime now.

"We need to get you to the hospital and get those wounds

dressed, Miss," the soldier said, as he gently led her to a waiting cart filled with casualties.

* * *

Richmond's industries and institutions were all equally hard hit by the explosion. Hundreds of workers died horrible deaths when factories such as the Acadia Sugar Refinery, the Dominion Textiles Cotton Factory, Nova Scotia Car Company, Richmond Printing Company, and Hillis & Sons Foundry were reduced to rubble. The Protestant Orphanage was also levelled, and most of the children, as well as the matron, were killed. None of the area's four churches — St. Joseph's, St. Mark's, Kaye Street Methodist Church, and Grove Presbyterian — was spared that day.

The schools were also ravaged. St. Joseph's on Gottingen, Bloomfield School on Agricola, and the Richmond School (also known as Roome Street School) were severely damaged.

Left: The rebuilt Richmond School as it existed in 2004.
Below: Richmond School students, before the explosion.

Survivors and volunteers searched the wreckage for days following the explosion.

However, fewer children died in the schools than out on the streets or at home that morning. Between 300 and 400 students were enrolled at Richmond School at the time. But because it had just switched over to the winter schedule, classes didn't start until 9:30 that day. As a result, rather than being in class, many of the children rushed down to the waterfront to get a look at the burning vessel. In all, eighty-four students from Richmond School perished. Bloomfield, which was closest to ground zero, was ravaged in the blast, and several students sustained injuries, but all 800 survived. St. Joseph's, however, lost a total of sixty-three students in the blast. Three girls were killed in the school, and another fifteen who were not in school that day perished. And since the boys didn't have classes until afternoon, many were either home or out on the streets. As a result, fifty-five boys from St. Joseph's died that day.

* * *

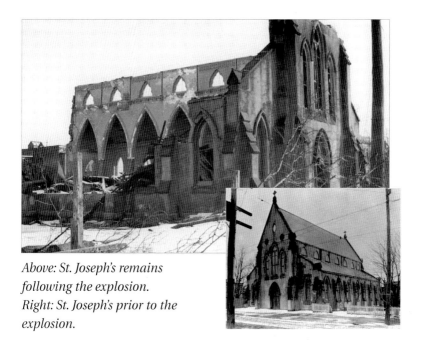

Above: St. Joseph's remains following the explosion.
Right: St. Joseph's prior to the explosion.

The students were in the midst of morning prayers at St. Joseph's when the two-storey building shuddered, and then there was a thunderous crash. The Sister leading the prayers screamed something about the Germans attacking. The ceiling began to sag and crack, and chunks of plaster rained down on the terrified girls. Eleanor Coleman's first thoughts were of her mother and her sisters, Babe and Nita, just down the street. If the Germans were attacking, what would happen to them?

The Sister managed to herd the girls out of the room just minutes before the ceiling came crashing down. As they picked their way through the rubble, they could hear shrieks and sobs coming from other parts of the building. The school was a shambles. The explosion had ripped off most of the roof, and the lower floors had collapsed like falling dominoes, leaving the grade eight students trapped between floors near the top of the building. The stairs had been ripped from their moorings, so the children were forced to climb out of

Many houses collapsed in on themselves following the blast, trapping many beneath rubble and debris.

windows and jump to the ground to escape. One of the nuns, who had been blinded by flying glass, led her students out of the wreckage by feel. Miraculously, only three girls were killed, but many, including a few of the nuns, were badly injured.

Once outside, Eleanor looked around for her brother Gerald, who had been serving in the morning mass next door. Not seeing him anywhere in the turmoil of the schoolyard, she set off for home by herself. The sights out on the street were horrifying. Almost every house on Russell Street had been reduced to rubble, and many were on fire. Mangled bodies lay in the street, and cries for help came from the ruins. George Oak, a neighbour from up the street who had a wooden leg, was crawling through the wreckage of his home. His wooden leg had been blown off in the explosion and his young daughter had been pinned beneath the chimney bricks. The sight of the fifty-eight-year-old calling out his daughter's name while frantically pawing through the ruins was pitiful. It seemed as though the whole world had been transformed into the hellish abyss of fire and brimstone the nuns and priests were always going on about.

As she approached her house, Eleanor felt sick. The Coleman's brand new house, like all the others along the street, was now nothing but a smouldering pile of debris. Gerald had raced home ahead of her and he and Nita were already digging among the piles of splintered boards and chunks of lath and plaster in search of their mother and sister. The cries of their baby sister coming from the wreckage compelled them to work faster. The heat and smoke from the surrounding fires was overwhelming, but the children barely noticed. They heaved beams and lifted sections of walls that would have been impossible for them to budge under normal circumstances. Finally, they lifted a portion of the kitchen wall to find their mother unconscious on the floor. A few feet away, sheltered beneath the kitchen sink, was Babe. She appeared to be unharmed, but their mother was in bad shape. Eleanor grabbed the baby,

Fire crews attempting to extinguish blazing buildings on Gottingen Street.

while Nita and Gerald lifted Frances from the wreckage. They decided to go back uphill toward the church, where they were certain they would find help. By then, Russell Street was an inferno, and smoke stung their eyes and seared their throats as they struggled up the steep slope to Gottingen Street.

When Frances Coleman regained consciousness, she was astonished to find herself on the sidewalk on Gottingen Street. The last thing she remembered was sitting at the kitchen table having coffee with her sister-in-law, while Babe played contentedly with her wooden blocks at their feet. After rushing around preparing breakfast and getting Vincent and the children out the door, Frances was enjoying the peaceful interlude. Suddenly, a terrible crack shattered the tranquility. Frances's sister-in-law jumped to her feet and cried, "Oh my God, the Germans are here!"

When Frances tried to move, a sharp pain shot through her back. Nita and Gerald hovered over her, their soot-smeared faces filled with worry. What on earth had happened? And why was she lying here on the cold sidewalk? Gerald explained that a ship had blown up in the harbour and the house had been demolished. Suddenly, Frances thought of her husband, Vincent. Was he okay? Another painful spasm gripped her, and everything went black again.

* * *

Meanwhile, at the Halifax County Academy, the students had just finished singing the morning hymn and were about to take their seats when the brick building rocked and shook as though swatted by a giant hand. This was followed by an ear-splitting roar. The windows shattered and girls shrieked as plaster and glass rained down around them. Evelyn Fox latched on to the chair in front of her and held on until the torrent died down. "The Germans must be shelling the school," she thought. Similar thoughts were shared by almost everyone in the city that morning. This wasn't too surprising, since only

*Anti-submarine nets were strung across the entrance of the harbour
each evening to prevent enemy vessels from entering under the cover
of darkness.*

the week before the headlines in a local paper read: "Toronto
Startled by a Report that the Huns had Landed and that Halifax,
St. John, and Ottawa were in Ruins and Quebec was Besieged!"
The city had been on alert for such an attack for months. Now,
it seemed, the assault had finally begun.

For several seconds after the blast, the entire assembly sat
perfectly still, waiting for another strike. When nothing further happened, the principal ushered everyone down the fire
escape to the schoolyard. As she stepped outside, Evelyn was
struck by the silence of the city. She had expected soldiers
to be swarming through the streets, guns at the ready. The
unnatural quiet was disturbing, as though the whole town
was holding its breath, waiting for the next blow to fall. One of
her classmates pointed to the smoke in the sky over the North
End and they all turned to see what looked to Evelyn like "a
grey mushroom on a thick pallid stalk, silver-edged, black
and purple lined, splendid but malignant, writhing evilly as it
climbed and spread. "

Chapter 4
SHOCK WAVES

Shortly after the explosion, casualties began pouring into Dr. George MacIntosh's home on Robie Street. The doctor, however, was on call at the hospital at the time. His wife, Clara, was still in her housecoat when people began arriving at the door.

Clara was head of the Lady's Division of the St. John's Ambulance Brigade in Halifax. The petite, energetic blond had a gift for organization, a talent that would be put to the test in the coming days.

Many of the wounded who showed up at the MacIntosh home were what Clara called "walking cases." Several of these individuals, however, collapsed from loss of blood as soon as they arrived at her door. Most were neighbours or patients of the doctor, but a few were from the North End. Lillian Griffin had walked all the way from the centre of the devastated area. Lillian had been on the third floor of a house near the foot of Kaye Street when the explosion occurred. Next thing she knew, she was lying in the street drenched in a black oily substance with a telegraph pole across her chest. When she arrived at Clara's door, she was a shocking sight. Her skin, hair, and clothes were completely black, and her coat was

A Halifax nurse manning one of the many ambulances kept busy in the aftermath of the explosion.

in tatters. Despite her appearance, Lillian wasn't badly hurt. What she needed more than anything, she told Clara, was a bath. Once the bath was run and Lillian was happily soaking, Clara asked the maid to wash the woman's clothes. As she gathered up the garments, the maid was astonished to see that like all the other items, Lillian's underwear was completely saturated with the black substance. And no matter how much she scrubbed, the grime just wouldn't wash out.

After Lillian was cleaned up and given a cup of tea, she was put to work sweeping up the glass and plaster covering the floors. Several of the men who had arrived at the door were busy boarding up windows, while Clara and the maid attended to the worst cases.

By the time Dr. MacIntosh arrived home at 9:45, the house was overflowing with casualties. They perched in the stairwell and spilled out into the kitchen, dining, and living rooms. Even the furnace room was packed with people seeking medical attention.

Shortly after 10:00 a.m., a soldier pounded on the door and briskly informed Clara that the magazine was on fire and she was to evacuate the house. Clara tried to explain that the

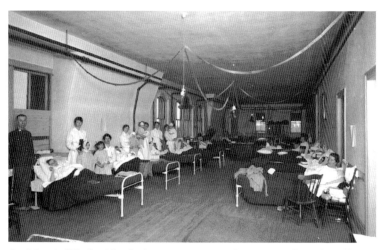

St. Mary's filled with victims as more survivors were found. Beds quickly became a rare luxury for many of the wounded and dying.

house was full of patients, many of whom couldn't be moved. But the soldier simply repeated the order and moved on to the next house. Fortunately, the open fields of the Commons were directly across the street from the MacIntosh residence. Many, however, were unable to walk and had to be carried the short distance. In order to make the patients more comfortable, Clara had the maid gather all the blankets and rugs in the house and spread them over the cold ground. After all, who knew how long they would be out there?

* * *

Hospitals and doctors' offices throughout Halifax and Dartmouth were quickly overwhelmed by the vast numbers of wounded and dying that morning. There were three major hospitals and several smaller medical facilities scattered throughout Halifax and Dartmouth at the time. All had sustained a certain amount of damage in the explosion — windows were smashed out, ceilings collapsed, and plaster and debris rained down on beds, operating tables, and equipment. To make matters worse, many of the hospitals were understaffed and ill equipped to begin with. There were only three X-ray machines in the entire city. And the newly opened Camp Hill Hospital — built as a convalescent facility for returned soldiers — contained no surgical equipment whatsoever. Even basic necessities such as hot water bottles were in short supply, as were morphine, anaesthetics, antiseptic, and sterilizing equipment. The shortage of equipment and supplies further complicated the already critical state of affairs.

* * *

Florence Murray had been up late studying the night before, and since she didn't have any classes that morning, she allowed herself the luxury of sleeping in. The twenty-three-year-old was in her fourth year of medical school at Dalhousie University. Her parents were living in Prince Edward Island at the time, so Florence boarded with a family near campus in the city's South End. She had just gotten out of bed when there was a deep rumble and crack that sounded "like all thunders rolled into one." The house shook violently. Windows shattered and china and pictures crashed to the floor. Certain an air raid attack was underway, she ran outside in her nightgown to find out what was happening. All along the street, doors were blown in and windows shattered. Although she still had no idea what had caused the blast, she was certain medical assistance would be needed.

Florence Murray was an intelligent, sensitive yet strong-willed, blue-eyed blond. The daughter of a Presbyterian minister and a school teacher, she had grown up in rural Nova Scotia at a time when career options for women were extremely limited. As she later wrote, "The only careers that I knew of open to girls were teaching, nursing, and stenography, none of which appealed to me. I wanted to do something different." What she wanted to be was a doctor. Several people

Part of Dalhousie's medical campus as it exists today.

tried to discourage her, including the principal of her college. "Instructors and students would hate having a woman in the class," they said. But Florence wasn't deterred, despite the fact that most Canadian universities didn't even accept women into their medical programs at the time. Fortunately, Dalhousie University was an exception, and in 1914 Florence passed the matriculation exam and was accepted into their medical program.

Like all nursing and medical students, Florence was eager to do whatever she could to aid the victims that morning. She dressed quickly and headed straight to the nearest drugstore to pick up bandages and iodine. The store was a shambles. The plate-glass window had blown in, the shelves were knocked to the floor, and the merchandise was buried in a thick crust of glass and plaster. Florence was rooting through the debris when a man arrived at the door with a woman in his arms. Both were bathed in blood.

"Can you help her?" the man asked.

The woman's face had been sliced open and an artery severed. Blood gushed uncontrollably from the wound. Florence helped the man get the woman slumped into a chair and examined the wound. She knew the hemorrhaging couldn't be stopped with iodine and bandages; the woman needed surgery. With trembling hands, Florence dressed the wound as well as she could and told the man to get the woman to a hospital as quickly as possible.

After gathering together what supplies she could find, Florence set off back down Robie Street. Her intention was to go to the Victoria General, the city's largest hospital, which was in the South End. But as she approached Camp Hill Hospital, she noticed a procession of carts, wagons, and automobiles pulling up to the front door and dropping off wounded. She decided to stop there.

* * *

While doctors, nurses, and volunteers all over town were struggling to save as many lives as possible that morning, city officials were attempting to restore order. The situation was dire. Fires raged out of control throughout the devastated area, and the fire department was in turmoil. Several of its members, including the fire chief, had been killed, and its only motorized pumper had been destroyed in the blast. The police force wasn't in much better shape. It lacked the training, equipment, and manpower to deal with a disaster of this magnitude. Added to this was the fact that 20,000 people were suddenly destitute, homeless, and in immediate need of shelter, food, clothing, and medical care.

Since Mayor Peter Martin happened to be out of town at the time, Deputy Mayor Henry Colwell found himself in the unenviable position of authority that day. Fortunately, the thirty-two-year-old alderman was up for the challenge. One thing Colwell had working in his favour was the fact that there were approximately 5,000 sailors and soldiers stationed in the city at the time. The military had the skills and the manpower to contain the damage, put out the fires, and conduct the

Soldiers worked around the clock searching for survivors in the wreckage of the city.

search and rescue operation. With this in mind, Colwell hurried over to military headquarters on Spring Garden Road to meet with Colonel W. E. Thompson.

Before long, armed guards were posted around the devastated area, and only those carrying official passes were permitted to enter. Furthermore, all vehicles of any kind were commandeered for transporting casualties to hospitals and bodies to the morgue. Throughout the crisis, soldiers performed above and beyond the call of duty. They worked around the clock, often risking their own lives to rescue others. They distributed blankets and food to the survivors, gave up their beds, and in many instances even gave the coats off their backs to others in need.

In order to cope with the full-scale medical emergency the city had on its hands, outside assistance was essential. But since the telephone and telegraph lines had been severed, Colwell wasn't able to make contact with anyone outside the city. Luckily, W. A. Duff, Assistant Chief Engineer of the Canadian Government Railway, happened to be in town at the time. When he discovered that all lines of communication were down and trains were unable to enter the city, he quickly set out for Rockingham. He intended to send a message to his general manager explaining the situation and requesting help. It took Duff a few tries before he managed to reach Rockingham. Once there, however, he was able to get through to the manager. The Canadian Government Railway responded immediately. Within hours, relief trains were being organized in several cities to transport doctors, nurses, and medical supplies to Halifax.

* * *

As the No. 10 train chugged cautiously towards the city, Colonel Phinney kept a sharp eye on the cloud of smoke billowing high above the North End. Twenty-five-year old Earle Caleb Phinney had been second in command of

Relief workers, including members of Harvard University's medical team, came from as far as the United States.

Relief trains continued to arrive in the city in the days and weeks following the explosion, carrying much-needed supplies and volunteers.

the Nova Scotia Highlanders 85th Battalion eight months earlier, when it had gained a reputation as an outstanding combat unit in the battle of Vimy Ridge. Phinney was credited for being cool and resourceful under fire in what was one of the bloodiest and most critical battles of the war. He survived Vimy unharmed; however, he was later wounded in another engagement and had recently been invalided home.

When the No. 10 rolled to a stop on the edge of the devastated area, everyone aboard fell silent. Where the thriving community of Richmond once stood, there was now nothing but hectares of blackened, smouldering rubble. Here and there the blazing remains of a factory or school loomed above the ruins. Everything else was flattened. A dense layer of smoke blotted out the sun, and an unnatural stillness hung over the ruins. Alongside the tracks, dozens of badly injured men, women, and children lay on boards, broken beds, doors, or whatever they could find. Minutes after the train stopped, hordes of desperate people emerged from the ruins and stumbled toward it, begging for help. Most were scantily clad, barefoot, and badly wounded. Phinney noted that all were "as black as if they had been shovelling coal." Those who couldn't walk were dragged along in blankets or pushed in wheelbarrows. The wounded pressed towels, pillows, or rags to injuries in an effort to staunch the flow of blood.

After a brief conference, Colonel Phinney and Conductor Gillespie decided the only thing to do was bring the victims aboard. Following Gillespie's orders, the men unloaded the baggage and mailbags in order to make room for as many as possible. The women raided the dining car and sleeping compartments in search of towels, table linens, bedding, or anything else that could be torn into strips for bandages. Once they'd loaded about 200 casualties aboard, Gillespie realized many wouldn't survive long without medical attention. One passenger volunteered to go out to look for a doctor. Shortly after the volunteer set out, however, another train with a doctor on board arrived at the scene.

Major Avery DeWitt was a physician at Camp Aldershot in the Annapolis Valley. The dark-haired thirty-six-year-old had been on his way to Halifax that morning to attend a meeting, but had grabbed his medical kit out of habit before leaving the house. As he surveyed the trainload of frightfully injured victims eyeing him hopefully, he was thankful he'd brought it along. He hadn't enough equipment or supplies to treat half the casualties on board, but at least the small amount of morphine he did have would ease the suffering of the worst cases.

Once Gillespie had things under control, Colonel Phinney organized a search and rescue party to go out into the ruins. By this time, soldiers and sailors were beginning to show up individually or in small groups. Many were returned soldiers who, like Phinney, had been invalided home. Some, Phinney noted, had only one arm or leg, yet this didn't stop them from volunteering for the rescue party. The men were split up into groups of half a dozen or so and instructed to work as systematically as possible.

"Concentrate on rescuing the survivors for the time being," Phinney ordered. "If there's no one in the house, let it burn."

In his time at the front, Colonel Phinney had witnessed

the most gruesome sights imaginable. He'd seen fully clothed bodies that had been blown to bits, and others that had every stitch of clothing torn off, but not so much as a mark on them. And he'd observed the look of determination on the faces of fallen comrades. But as battle-hardened as he was, he wasn't prepared for what he would encounter in the ruins that day. Recovering the bodies of men, women, and children who had been dismembered, disfigured, beheaded, or mangled beyond recognition was, for many of the returned soldiers, much more disturbing than seeing casualties on the battlefield.

One of the most peculiar cases Phinney dealt with was a young boy who was fully conscious and quite calm, despite the fact that he had a rivet driven into his right eye. In addition to the rivet, a large chunk of iron plating from the *Mont-Blanc* was sunk into his chest, and another in his right thigh. The metal, which had been searing hot when it penetrated the boy's flesh, had cauterized the wounds so there was no bleeding. Phinney, however, felt the boy's chances of survival were very slim.

One of the passengers from the No. 10 who joined the

Heavy snowfall in the days after the explosion hindered the rescue efforts of the soldiers and volunteers.

The Dingle Tower, designed by Andrew Cobb, still stands above Sir Sandford Fleming Park.

rescue party that morning was Andrew Cobb. At forty-one years of age, Cobb was one of the most sought-after architects in the Maritimes. Prior to the war, his career had been soaring. He had won several prestigious contracts throughout the region and his designs had received glowing reviews. Recently, however, the war had begun to put a damper on things. Although Halifax had prospered as a result of the war, commissions for the type of buildings Cobb was interested in designing had begun to dry up. However, he still had more than enough work to keep him busy.

Four people were trapped beneath the first house Cobb and his team came across. The entire house had collapsed on a man and his wife and a mother and son. All four were conscious, and they pleaded for help and shouted directions to the men, who worked feverishly to free them. It was a Herculean task. Large sections of roof and walls, too heavy for the men to lift, had to be torn apart before they could be removed. But with nothing other than their bare hands to

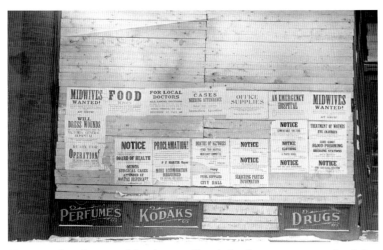

Damaged or destroyed businesses lined the downtown stretch of the once-lively Barrington Street.

work with, the going was slow. To make matters worse, the rescue party was distracted by what was going on at the next house. It had caught fire with four children trapped inside. The parents and several others were frantically trying to rescue the children. But it was clear from the intensity of the fire, and the children's cries, that they were being burned alive.

Dealing with the fires that sprang up following the explosion was one of the greatest challenges rescue workers faced. Many reported that the most psychologically disturbing aspect of their task was being unable to save victims trapped in burning buildings. In a letter to his commanding officer, Lieutenant Herbert Percival, RNR stated, "Many badly injured were pulled from under houses which had collapsed and I am sorry to say a few had to be abandoned as the houses crashed down in flames. There were no available means of extinguishing the fire."

After hours of back-breaking labour, Cobb and the others finally managed to free the family from the wreckage. The man was unharmed. His wife, however, was badly wounded. Her face had been severely lacerated and she had lost an eye.

The other woman and her son only sustained minor cuts and bruises, but were traumatized by the experience.

Once the family was rescued, Andrew Cobb was physically and emotionally drained. At 1:00 p.m., he left the others and set off for his office on Barrington Street. Although the sun was still high in the sky, the thick layer of smoke shrouding the North End made it seem much later in the day. Getting around, even on foot, was complicated by the tangles of downed wires, poles, and debris covering the roads. And the sight of corpses — many of which appeared to have drowned — scattered throughout the ruins was distressing, to say the least.

While Andrew Cobb was making his way to Barrington Street, Conductor Gillespie was preparing to take the No. 10 back to Rockingham, where he hoped to make contact with his superiors to find out what should be done with his trainload of casualties.

Chapter 5
TOO HORRIBLE TO DESCRIBE

The search and rescue efforts were just getting underway on the morning of the disaster, when the city's shell-shocked citizens were rocked by the news of another impending crisis: the military magazine at Wellington Barracks was thought to be on fire and another explosion imminent. The large military complex was situated just above the Dockyard on Barrington Street, and was home to the 76th Regiment, a composite battalion made up of men whose main duty was to guard the waterfront and the town. The compound consisted of a cluster of buildings, including the enlisted men's quarters, officers' quarters, married quarters, and the magazine, a small storage building stockpiled with munitions.

The battalion was in the midst of morning inspection in the parade square when the explosion occurred. Being so close to the harbour, the garrison was hit hard. Once the barrage of shrapnel let up, the place was in chaos. The parade square, where only minutes earlier rows of perfectly-groomed soldiers stood at attention awaiting inspection, was now strewn with casualties, broken rifles, backpacks, and chunks of

Above: Wellington Barracks prior to the explosion.
Right: The crumbling interior of the barracks in the aftermath of the blast.

debris. Although the brick exteriors of the two-storey buildings were strong enough to withstand the explosion, the interiors were in ruins. According to one witness, the officers' mess looked like "a cardboard box which had been stepped on." And the married quarters were a shambles. The roofs were smashed in, the windows shattered, and the walls looked as though they'd been hit with a wrecking ball. Stoves were knocked over and fires blazed throughout the complex. Many of the women and children, including the colonel's wife, were seriously wounded and in desperate need of medical attention.

THE
DEC. 6
1917
HALIFAX
EXPLOSION
HURLED THIS
1140 LB ANCHOR
SHAFT 2.35 MILES
FROM THE S.S. MONT
BLANC TO THIS PARK.

A piece of Mont-Blanc's *anchor, mounted where it landed after the explosion.*

Among those injured was the orderly officer, Lieutenant Balcom, whose thigh had been shattered by a piece of shrapnel. With Balcom out of commission, Lieutenant Charles MacLennan assumed command. MacLennan had all those who were able — about fifteen men out of 100 — fall in. The troop did a quick tour of the garrison, checking for fires and taking stock of the damage.

The magazine, a small building surrounded by an iron fence, was situated in the corner of the compound closest to the harbour. MacLennan noted that it appeared to be extensively damaged. A two-metre chunk of steel plating off the *Mont-Blanc* had soared through the air and landed on the iron picket fence, leaving a gaping hole large enough for a person to squeeze through. Worse, the door of the building was blown in and the roof partially torn off. MacLennan set a detail of men to work clearing debris from the magazine, and continued his inspection tour.

Attached to the magazine was the furnace room, which had also been hammered by the blast. When MacLennan stuck his head in the door, his heart skipped a beat. Coals had spilled from the furnace onto the wooden floor and ignited. Flames flickered up the walls, alarmingly close to a large open duct leading directly to the munitions storage area. The situation was critical. MacLennan snatched a nearby fire extinguisher and began battling the blaze. After several tense minutes, he succeeded in dousing the fire. But as a result, a huge cloud of smoke and steam billowed out through the hole in the roof and was visible to everyone in the area. The men clearing debris from the magazine were the first to catch sight of the smoke. Thinking the building was on fire and the munitions about to explode, they dropped what they were doing and ran for their lives. Outside the garrison fence, a group of civilians noticed the commotion. Everyone who lived in the area knew this was the military magazine. So the sight of panic-stricken soldiers fleeing from the burning building terrified them.

Word that the magazine was about to blow spread through the city like wildfire. Hordes of already traumatized people ran for their lives, leaving countless victims trapped beneath the ruins. Soldiers were dispatched to knock on doors and warn everyone to leave the area and head for open spaces. Before long, Citadel Hill, the Commons, and Point Pleasant Park were crowded with terrified souls waiting for the next blow to fall.

When Charles MacLennan looked out to see the men from his work detail scrambling to get through the hole in the fence, he instinctively dropped the extinguisher and began to follow. But there was such a crowd trying to squeeze through the opening that he couldn't get near it.

"What's all the panic about?" he asked a bystander.

"The roof of the magazine is on fire!" the man replied.

MacLennan paused for a moment to consider the situation. There was really no point in running, he realized. If

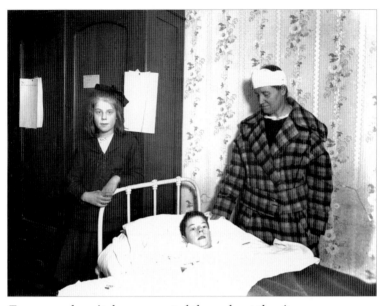

Temporary hospitals were erected throughout the city.

the magazine were to blow up, he'd be killed anyway. He decided to climb onto the roof to assess the situation. While the magazine was damaged, it didn't appear to be on fire. By the time he climbed back down, the crowd in the street had vanished. Although he, too, was tempted to run, the lieutenant decided to remain at his post and do whatever he could to avert a second explosion. His sentry, a youth by the name of Eisnor, had also remained on duty. The boy suffered from the worst case of shellshock MacLennan had ever seen. He had great difficulty controlling his facial muscles or his hands. Nevertheless, Eisnor was determined to do his bit to save the magazine. He got another fire extinguisher and worked at keeping the flames under control, while MacLennan went and rounded up more recruits. The men worked feverishly, clearing out the magazine and hosing down the furnace room for several hours before the crisis was finally averted.

* * *

Over in Dartmouth, Dr. Miner S. Dickson was in the midst of amputating a badly mangled arm when the warning of a second explosion reached him. With the help of his niece, Annie Anderson, he managed to move the patient and operating table out into the street, where he successfully completed the amputation and continued to stitch up wounds until they got word that it was safe to move back inside.

Annie, a medical student at Dalhousie, was boarding with her uncle at the time. The fifty-year-old doctor had been battling stomach cancer and was sick in bed when the explosion occurred. Shortly afterwards, the house was inundated with wounded and dying seeking medical attention. When Annie went up to check on her uncle, she found him buried beneath a layer of glass and plaster. Fortunately, his only injuries were a few minor cuts. When Annie explained what had happened and told him about the crowd downstairs, Dickson insisted on getting dressed and going down to tend to the desperate multitude filling the house.

Most of the injuries Annie and Dr. Dickson dealt with that day were head gashes and cuts around the eyes. One of the

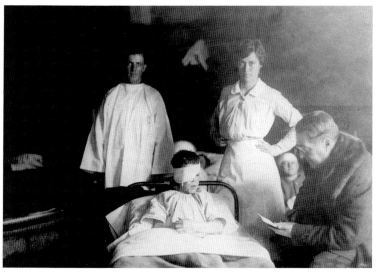

Eye wounds were among some of the most common injuries sustained.

worst cases they attended to was a woman who was a clerk in a nearby shop. The store's plate-glass window had shattered in the blast, and a glass dagger had slashed the woman's cheek and sliced into her windpipe. By the time she arrived at the doctor's office, the wound was "oozing froth."

Later that afternoon, Annie accompanied Dr. Dickson to the Nova Scotia Hospital, where the pair worked non-stop until late into the night. Annie helped dress wounds and clean up the patients, many of whom she noted "were covered with oily black soot that ruined the furniture." She was struck by the fortitude of the people she tended to that day. In spite of the fact that there was neither chloroform nor hypodermics to ease the pain, "even little children made no fuss when their injuries were dressed."

The next day, a VON by the name of Miss Bishop stayed in their office to care for any injured persons who called, while Annie and Dr. Dickson went into the community to tend to cases that couldn't be moved. Many of those they visited were living in deplorable conditions. In several instances, they found two or three families crammed together in one or two rooms. With all the windows boarded up, it was difficult to see where you were going or what you were doing most of the time, but they persevered. After three days of working non-stop, Dr. Dickson collapsed. Annie put him to bed, but two days later he was back at it again.

* * *

While the rest of the city was in turmoil over a possible second explosion, Frances Coleman regained consciousness to find herself jammed into the back of an open wagon along with several other wounded people. As the wagon lurched along, each rut they hit sent up a chorus of groans. Frances was grateful when they finally pulled to a stop in front of Camp Hill Hospital. After they lifted her from the wagon, the stretcher-bearers carried her inside and set her down among hundreds of others. As she glanced around, the enormity of what had occurred began to sink in. Sobs and moans echoed through the wards. And the foyer and corridors were so packed with horribly wounded people that it was almost impossible for the nurses and stretcher-bearers to move around without stumbling over a body.

After the wagon had departed with their mother on-board, the Coleman children stood on the corner shivering. Babe was cold and hungry and beginning to fuss. They had to get her out of the cold and find something to feed her soon. They couldn't go home; it was nothing but a burning pile of rubble. The school and church were in the same condition. To make matters worse, they had no idea where their father was, nor did they know if their mother was going to survive her injuries. When Eleanor began to cry, Nita realized she had to take charge.

"We'll go to Grandmother O'Toole's," she decided.

As they set out for Edward Street in the South End, Nita prayed that when they got there, their grandmother's house would still be standing.

* * *

While the Coleman children were making their way over to their grandmother's, Ralph Proctor was trying to figure out how he'd ever manage to dig his car out from beneath the heap of rubble under which it was buried. His father had bought Ralph the new Model T when he arrived home from France a few months earlier. Ralph was a member of the 85th Battalion, which had gone to France under the command of Colonel Phinney two months prior to the Battle of Vimy Ridge. Since the battalion had not had any combat experience, it was never intended to play a fighting role in the battle. According to author John Boileau, "The 85th was to follow the leading troops, carry ammunition, build dugouts, dig communication trenches, and clear wire entanglements."

Ralph Proctor, prior to being injured in the Battle of Vimy Ridge.

However, after two battalions were wiped out while attempting to take Hill 145, the highest and most heavily defended elevation on the ridge, two companies of the 85th were thrust into the fray.

As the troops advanced on enemy lines that bleak Easter Monday, they were hammered by a barrage of mortar and gunfire. Against all odds, the inexperienced recruits of the 85th took their objective within an hour. But the cost was tremendous. Fifty-six of those who marched into battle that day were killed, and close to 300 were wounded.

Nineteen-year-old Ralph Proctor was among the casualties. As his company advanced that morning, shrapnel ripped into Ralph's spine and right thigh, bringing him down. As he lay in the bloodied muck of no man's land, a German came along and bayoneted him in the chest to be sure he was dead. When the medics retrieved his broken body and took him back to the field hospital, they discovered that his right leg was shattered and two vertebrae were crushed. Worse, the bayonet had punctured one of his lungs.

For the next few months, Ralph was confined to a hospital in France until he recovered enough to be shipped home. During that time, he got word that his older brother, Athol, had been killed in another clash just one month after the Battle of Vimy Ridge.

Eight months later, the pain in Ralph's back and leg was still excruciating and he had difficulty breathing. His doctors

The Nova Scotia Highlanders, Canada's 85th battalion, of which Ralph was a member.

had forbidden him to do any lifting whatsoever. But he was determined not to let his disabilities stop him. Once he was able, he started helping out in the office of the family business, a grocery on Barrington Street. That morning, he had dressed in his uniform and gone down to the office to get caught up on some paperwork.

After the blast, Ralph had attended to a few employees who had sustained flesh wounds before rushing home to check on his family and get his car. Since he was among the few people in the city with an automobile, he knew his services would be needed to transport casualties to the hospital. His heart sank when he arrived home to find his new car buried beneath the rubble of the garage. As he set to work heaving and dragging beams and boards from around the car, his doctor's orders not to lift any weight crossed his mind. But he pushed the thought aside and carried on.

Those vehicles that were still operational after the explosion were repurposed to transport victims.

Once Ralph had cleared enough of the rubble that he could move the vehicle, another obstacle presented itself. The chimney from a neighbouring house had collapsed into the street and piles of bricks blocked the driveway. Ralph was out clearing the bricks from the road when some soldiers came along and gave him a hand.

Shortly after setting out, Ralph came across a man staggering down the street clutching his arm. The arm was all but completely severed from the shoulder. A mere shred of flesh was all that kept it attached. Blood gushed from the wound and the man was dazed and weak. After helping him into the car, Ralph set off for Camp Hill Hospital, stopping to pick up others along the way. By the time they pulled up in front of the hospital, the car was loaded with casualties.

After dropping off his first load, Ralph turned around and went back for another. Driving through the devastated area was hazardous. Shrapnel, debris, timbers, dead horses, overturned carts, and downed telephone poles littered the deeply-rutted dirt roads. As the car bounced and jolted along, the pain in his back intensified. To make matters worse, almost every house in the devastated area was ablaze by then, and the thick smoke blanketing the area made breathing difficult. At one point, overcome by a coughing spasm, Ralph clasped his handkerchief over his mouth. When he pulled it away, he was alarmed to see that it was spattered with blood. The wound in his lung had opened and was hemorrhaging. But this was no time to worry about himself. There were hundreds of critically injured and dying people in urgent need of medical care.

The array of injuries suffered by Ralph's passengers that day was astonishing and often heart wrenching. One fellow's jugular vein had been pierced by a stiletto of glass. Another's neck was skewered by a large pointed stick of wood. He found one young girl lying in the street, her naked body studded with glass and covered in blood from hundreds of lacerations. But it was the five-year-old with a broken spine that bothered Ralph the most. He later described the sights he saw in the ruins that day as being worse than anything he'd seen in France.

"Over there," he said. "You don't see women and children all broken to pieces."

* * *

Rockhead was one of the hardest hit hospitals in the city that day. Since it was situated on a bluff overlooking the Narrows, it took the full brunt of the blast. Although the reinforced concrete walls remained standing, the building was a wreck. Doors were blown off, and the large windows were shattered. What's more, the roof had caved in, and glass and plaster showered down on the beds and floors. With no roof or windows to keep out the cold, the frozen pipes had burst and torrents of water sprayed everywhere. Shortly after the blast, casualties began streaming into the hospital. Before long, every square inch was crammed with desperate individuals seeking medical attention. When there was no more room in the wards and corridors, the patients were laid out

Ambulances brought a steady influx of survivors to the St. Mary's temporary hospital.

on the office floors.

Luckily, the eighty convalescent soldiers occupying the beds at the time were relatively unharmed. Like their counterparts at Camp Hill Hospital, they gave up their beds to those in greater need without a second thought. Those who were able set to work nailing boards and tarpaper over the shattered windows, cleaning up the plaster and glass, and moving the beds from the top floor down to the ground floor.

While Camp Hill, the Victoria General, and other hospitals in the city were inundated with volunteers that day, Josephine and Helen Crichton were the only ones to venture all the way out to Rockhead. Until the two Dalhousie undergraduates showed up, Dr. Bruce Almon and his assistant struggled to keep up with the flood of patients on their own. When the girls asked how they could help, Dr. Almon instructed them to bathe and dress the minor wounds, but to leave the serious ones alone.

"They're better with the blood congealed," he said.

From the time they arrived until they left the next afternoon, Josephine and Helen never stopped. They dressed wounds, assisted the doctors, and tried to keep the patients warm the only way they could: by serving hot cups of tea and passing out warm bricks for the beds. The girls were astonished at the selflessness of their patients. Everyone, it seemed, was far more concerned about the welfare of others than about themselves.

As she sat among the crowd waiting to have her wounds dressed, Catherine James shivered uncontrollably and rubbed her bare arms in an effort to warm up. It was so cold in the roofless building that you could see your breath and she was still wearing nothing but the thin cotton dress she'd had on when the explosion occurred. Catherine's head was throbbing, and the sound of hammering and babies crying only

Prior to the explosion, the Victoria General Hospital, like Rockwood and Camp Hill, held many convalescent soldiers.

Nurses worked tirelessly preparing bandages and supplies.

made it worse. She idly watched the two young volunteers rushing around cleaning and dressing wounds. She noted that the girls had kept their coats and hats on, and they walked on their heels through the pools of water on the floor so as not to get their shoes soaked. After a time, one of the girls noticed Catherine and brought over a cup of tea.

As she gratefully sipped the steaming liquid, she wondered where Jack was and what they would do now that their house had been destroyed. Neither she nor her husband had family in the city they could stay with. Her father lived in Newfoundland, and Jack's only family in the province was a brother who lived down in Mahone Bay.

After what seemed like hours, the doctor finally got around to examining Catherine's wounds. Her face was badly lacerated, he said, and would require stitches.

"I'm afraid we've got nothing for the pain, so this may sting a bit," he said.

Catherine gritted her teeth and tried not to cry out as the needle jabbed into her flesh.

Chapter 6
EXODUS

Fred Longland thought the resounding boom of the explosion heralded "the end of the world." As he later told a friend, "I felt as though I'd been hit in the face with a big flat board." But he was one of the fortunate ones who managed to take cover and survived the blast unharmed. Many of his crewmates weren't so lucky.

By about 11:00 a.m., some semblance of order had been restored on the *Niobe*, and Fred was detailed to take a platoon out to search the streets and undertakers for dead sailors. He and his crew were told to watch for the distinctive bell-bottomed trousers of the navy uniform. Whenever they saw a pair, they were to dig out the body and lay it aside for pickup. It was a gruesome task. The carnage in the streets was horrendous. After hours of the grim search for fallen comrades, Fred was sick at heart and returned to the *Niobe* for a badly needed drink in the wardroom. Just as he sat down, however, a commander came looking for him.

"There is a man in Victoria [General] Hospital emergency ward, badly hurt, and in his extremity keeps on calling out your name," the commander informed him.

Since he had just arrived in town that morning, Fred couldn't imagine who even knew he was here.

* * *

After the initial shock of the explosion had passed, students at the Halifax County Academy were dismissed. Evelyn Fox left the school with her classmates, Patsy and Rose, who also travelled to the city by train. Initially, Evelyn assumed that the explosion that rocked the school had been caused by a German shell, and that the Academy was the only building affected by the blast. But as the girls headed north, it became increasingly clear that her assumption was wrong. All along Brunswick Street, windows were shattered and doors blown off hinges. And everyone they met along the way, Evelyn noted, seemed in a strange, "trance-like state."

When they arrived at the Alexandra School, Evelyn went in to let her father know that classes had been dismissed and that she was on her way to the station. Being further north than the Academy, the Alexandra School had been hit much harder. Evelyn was surprised to find her father in a classroom where "shreds of green blinds flapped at paneless windows, or were strewn across the floor where broken desks lay upon their sides, and slashed books and papers (many impaled upon long glass stilettos) mingled with inches-deep plaster and glass."

Mr. Fox was in the midst of bandaging a gash on a student's hand when she stuck her head in the door. He seemed relieved to see her.

"Douglas is all right," he said. "He stopped here on his way back to barracks to report for special duty."

Until that moment, it hadn't occurred to Evelyn that a member of her family, or anyone else, might have been hurt or even killed in the blast. Seeing the bewildered look on his daughter's face, Mr. Fox realized she had no idea what had occurred.

Few homes in the North End of the city were left unscathed.

"A munition ship blew up in the Narrows," he explained. Although this clarified things somewhat, she had yet to grasp the extent of the disaster.

Evelyn promised to wait for her father at the train station and left him to finish patching up his wounded students. On their way out the door, the girls ran into Hazel, another friend from Bedford.

By the time Evelyn and her friends reached North Street, the terrible nature of the catastrophe had begun to sink in. "On North Street the houses were completely shattered, barely standing and utterly deserted," Evelyn later wrote. The normally bustling intersection next to the train station was now unnaturally quiet. "A few women on foot, some weeping, some plainly beyond tears" passed by, followed by a few horse-drawn carts loaded with refugees and others transporting casualties to the hospital.

The stately King Edward Hotel, which stood directly across from the station, was a wreck. The windows had all been blown out and ragged bits of curtains flapped in the breeze. The station, through which Evelyn had passed only a few short hours ago, had also been hard hit. Its red brick façade

The Richmond Terminal was completely destroyed by the explosion.

withstood the blast relatively intact, but the glass and iron canopy covering the tracks and platforms had collapsed, killing several people and burying the tracks and battered railway cars in debris. But from where the girls stood, the building appeared relatively unscathed. Hazel decided to pop in and check the schedule to see if they might catch an earlier train home. When she returned a few minutes later, she looked as though she'd seen a ghost.

"What happened? What did you find out?" Evelyn asked.

"I couldn't get down," Hazel replied, her voice trembling. "There's a dead man lying across the stairs."

Not long after Hazel's macabre discovery, four soldiers came tearing down the street shouting, "Fire! Wellington Barracks Magazine is on fire! Move south, into the open! Everybody south!" Alarmed, Patsy, Rose, and Hazel took off immediately. But Evelyn was torn between obeying her father's request to wait for him at the station and the military command to move south. When the girls realized she wasn't behind them, they turned back. After some persuasion, she was convinced to follow the military command.

Before long, the girls found themselves perched among hundreds of others on the steep eastern slope of Citadel

Hill. The cold breeze on the hill made Evelyn shiver. As she eyed the crowd, she was grateful that she'd grabbed her coat before leaving the school that morning. Several people wore nothing but light dresses, underwear, or pyjamas. Some were barefoot, others shuffled along in bedroom slippers. Gulls wheeled overhead, their raucous cries puncturing the unnatural silence of the crowd. Up there, you had a panoramic view of the city and harbour. That day, however, the view was marred by great pillars of black smoke rising above the North End. But what was missing from the scene was even more disturbing.

"It's gone," someone whispered. "The refinery, it's gone."

A shudder of disbelief rippled through the crowd. The Acadia Sugar Refinery, a massive fifteen-storey red-brick structure that had dominated the skyline to the north, had been reduced to nothing but a pile of rubble. Suddenly, the Citadel seemed much too close to the munition ships and military magazines. People began to talk about heading further west. And before long, a column of horse-drawn carts,

Temporary tent shelters were erected on the Commons, near the Citadel.

Virtually nothing remained of the Acadia Sugar refinery.

wagons, and automobiles loaded with shell-shocked individuals was snaking its way across the city and out along St. Margaret's Bay Road. All thoughts of meeting her father vanished as Evelyn and her friends fell in with the mass exodus.

After they'd walked for what seemed like hours, the girls were tired and hungry. They decided they'd gone far enough. Many of the refugees had stopped and were crowded around small fires in a field beside the road. A tall, thin soldier with a friendly face invited the girls to share his fire. Laurence had just returned from France. He had sustained a bad foot wound in combat and had been invalided home. That morning, he had been in Camp Hill Hospital, and like the other convalescent soldiers had given up his bed to make room for those in greater need.

"But where will you sleep tonight?" Evelyn asked.

"I'll manage okay," he replied. "Many's the night I've slept out in my greatcoat."

Evelyn didn't find this very reassuring. She thought of her older brother, Ashford, who was over in France. How many nights had he spent in a muddy field or trench with nothing but his greatcoat to protect him from the elements?

Exodus

* * *

In the woods off Lady Hammond Road, Ada Moore was still reeling from the shock of witnessing the ruins of her house burn to the ground with her four youngest children trapped inside. What's more, she hadn't been able to find her four older children, and had no idea if they or her husband, Charles, were dead or alive. At that point, however, Ada was barely aware of the fact that half of her family was missing and the other half dead.

Following the disaster, many survivors who were in a deep state of shock wandered about, completely unaware of where they were or what was going on around them. Among these "disoriented souls" was a young girl who happened to be in the midst of dressing when the explosion occurred. As Dr. David Fraser Harris reported, the girl was "later found wandering towards an open space, valise in hand, wearing only her corsets. When others tried to help her, she suddenly realized her state of undress, sat down, and took out a pair of green silk stockings and white satin shoes from her case, and then continued on her way." Others were seen walking through the streets completely naked.

Survivors wandered the streets, many in shock and severely wounded.

Survivors from the Africville community in the North End.

As Ada stared despondently into the fire, a man came around and warned everyone that a second explosion was imminent and that they should clear out of the area. Terrified by this news, the refugees collected their few meagre possessions and set out for Rockingham. Ada plodded along numbly after the crowd. She was barely aware of the cold, despite the fact that all she had on over her underclothes was the sweater the woman in Richmond had tossed over her shoulders. After a time, a horse-drawn wagon carrying several besmirched, hollow-eyed survivors came along and offered her a lift.

* * *

While most people were desperately fleeing the North End in fear of a second explosion, Dean John Llwyd was rushing through the smoke and raging fires in the ravaged area to offer assistance. John Plummer Derwent Llwyd was the dean of All Saints Cathedral in the South End. That morning, Llwyd was in the midst of reading the Morning Prayer in the chapel when he felt the earth tremble beneath his feet. "A German shell!" he thought. He paused and looked up at the congregation. There were only three worshippers in the chapel that morning:

his wife Marie, and two other women. A few seconds passed before Llwyd cleared his throat and picked up where he'd left off. Suddenly, an earth-shattering roar drowned out his words. The massive stone building shuddered and each of the large windows lining the north side blew in, showering glass down on the pews. The women gasped and shrieked and Llwyd felt his knees go weak. He feared the building was going to come tumbling down, crushing them all to death. In all his fifty-six years, he had never experienced anything so terrifying.

When the furor died down, he ran to the doorway. The solid oak north doors were torn from their hinges. He looked out to see a cloud of yellowish-grey smoke that resembled "a huge flower unfolding" in the sky to the north.

After a few minutes, Llwyd returned to his congregation.

"It's all over, it must have been a munition explosion at some point north," he said in what he hoped was a reassuring tone. "We can go on and finish our service."

But the women were visibly shaken. Marie's hat, he noticed, had been blown off her head and lay on the floor near the altar. After a few perfunctory prayers, he ended the service and the little group filed outside, blinking in the bright sunshine.

After taking Marie home, Dean Llwyd decided to head downtown to find out what had caused the blast. He was certain there would be casualties, and wanted to offer whatever assistance he could. On Spring Garden Road, Llwyd ran into Mr. Hewat, a member of his congregation who had just come in on the train from Truro. Hewat was clearly upset. The explosion, he said, had actually lifted the train from the tracks. The passengers had been forced to disembark at some point before Richmond and walk through the devastated area. Hewat's voice quivered as he tried to describe the sights he'd seen in the North End.

"Everywhere houses razed to the ground," he said. "Buildings of considerable size, mere heaps of bricks. Fire has started and the wounded and dying are lying around in twos and threes."

When he arrived in the devastated area, Dean Llwyd couldn't believe his eyes. The entire area looked as though it had endured months of bombardment. The skeletal remains of a factory, a wall or two of a house, and the odd telephone pole were about the only things still standing in some areas. Bits and pieces of furniture stuck out from the piles of rubble, but for the most part, everything was smashed beyond recognition. Fires raged throughout the area, and mangled, charred corpses were everywhere. Smoke stung the cleric's eyes, and the stench of burning flesh nauseated him. Nothing in his sheltered background had prepared him for this.

He passed streams of walking wounded in tattered, bloody clothing. Many groped along blindly. Some had limbs missing or dangling uselessly from sockets. All were in a state of shock. Several individuals warned Llwyd about another explosion and told him to get out of the area. But he continued on until he came upon a group of soldiers and a Catholic priest digging casualties out of the ruins. He joined the rescue party and assisted in the taking out of a number of "poor crushed and mangled forms." He felt that many of those taken from the ruins would never survive the trip to the hospital.

The victims were being transported to the hospital ship USS *Old Colony*, which had been anchored off the south end of Dartmouth that morning. The vessel had survived the blast unscathed, and had immediately dispatched her boats, filled with blue jackets, to assist in the search and rescue effort. At about 1:00 p.m. *Old Colony* was brought over and docked astern of the *Niobe*. The Naval hospital at Pier 2 had been destroyed in the blast, so its patients were transferred to *Old Colony*, which could accommodate 150. The remaining beds were soon filled with men, women, and children from the devastated area.

After a few dozen corpses had been pulled from the wreckage, the commanding officer approached Llwyd and asked his advice about what should be done with them. The cleric suggested removing them from the ruins and laying them out

The USS Old Colony *hospital ship.*

side by side for identification and pickup. Before long, the rescue party had more than thirty bodies lined up on the side of the road. Many of the victims had been decapitated — their heads and sometime even the shoulders blown clean off. Others had limbs torn off, skulls bashed in, and great gashes on the torsos. One remarkable phenomenon was the number of dead that had been stripped of every stitch of clothing, but didn't have a mark on their bodies.

Every now and then the rescue workers heard the shrill whinnying of horses in distress. At first, they assumed the sound came from the dozens of spooked horses charging through the streets, many still hitched to wagons. (The soldiers had already been forced to shoot several injured horses and move them off the streets so as not to impede the flow of traffic carrying the wounded to the hospitals.) Eventually, however, the whinnying grew more insistent. Since the sound was distracting the men from the task at hand, the commanding officer sent a man off to investigate. Before long, the soldier returned and reported that he'd discovered a stable full of horses trapped in the ruins with fires closing in all around them. Unable to free the animals himself, he'd come back for help. Troubled by the news of animals in danger, several of the men dropped what they were doing and were about to rush off to rescue the horses. But the commanding officer ordered them back to work. It was more important to save human lives, he said, than those of animals. A few soldiers were ordered to go and see what they could do about the animals, while the rest went back to work.

When the men returned, their grimy faces were animated for the first time that day. All the horses had been freed, they reported triumphantly. Although it was a small victory in a day filled with so much tragedy, the news bolstered the men's spirits. They returned to their arduous duty with renewed energy.

After four hours of difficult search and rescue work, Dean Llwyd was drained. He requested permission to take a sergeant down to City Hall with him to find out what was to be done with the bodies that were quickly accumulating.

Llywd arrived at City Hall just as a meeting between Deputy Mayor Henry Colwell, Lieutenant-Governor MacCallum Grant, and the members of City Council was wrapping up. During the meeting, six committees were struck, including transportation, distribution of food and clothing, disposal of the dead, finance, and shelter for the homeless.

Prior to the disaster, the city had suffered from a serious housing shortage. Now, with thousands more suddenly homeless, housing was critical. The committee decided that any undamaged public buildings, such as the theatre, the Academy of Music, and all parish halls would be converted into temporary shelters. In addition, several organizations such as the Salvation Army and the Knights of Columbus, among others, had offered the use of their quarters for this purpose.

Disposal of the dead was another pressing issue. The huge number of casualties had quickly overwhelmed the city's few private funeral parlours, and it was essential that a temporary morgue be set up to deal with the excess. Colwell called on former mayor Robert MacIlreith to assist with this task. MacIlreith had been mayor when the *Titanic* had gone down

Above: The Hydrostone neighbourhood was built following the explosion to house the many displaced survivors.
Right: Hydrostone neighbourhood houses as they exist today.

five years earlier. Hundreds of the victims had been brought to Halifax for identification and burial. From that experience, MacIlreith had learned a great deal about handling such matters.

His first task was to find a suitable building in which to house a mortuary. After scouting out a few schools, MacIlreith decided that its size and location made the Chebucto Road School the best choice for a temporary morgue. The building needed several repairs and modifications, however, before it would be operational. Once again, the city turned to the military, requesting a detail of men to convert the school.

Another thing MacIlreith had learned from the *Titanic* disaster was that it was essential to follow proper forensic identification procedures in situations such as this. To make identification easier, each body recovered from the ruins was to be tagged, with the street name and, if possible, the house number where the body had been found, marked on the labels. In addition, any personal effects discovered on or near

Personal effects of unidentified male victim, on display at the Maritime Museum of the Atlantic.

the bodies that might help identify them were also collected and tagged.

* * *

Once the issue of the mortuary was settled, Dean Llwyd went home to clean up before heading over to Camp Hill Hospital. The hours of strenuous labour in the ruins had drained him, but as dean of All Saints Cathedral, it was his duty to comfort the victims. Llwyd was much more in his element in the hospital than out in the streets. As a man of the cloth, he had spent a great deal of time in hospitals, and he usually found these visits rewarding. Today, however, Llwyd found the scene at Camp Hill heart-rending. He felt certain that the sights he witnessed that day would haunt him forever.

* * *

A hundred kilometres away, in the town of Kentville, Dr. Willis Moore was preparing to make a house call when he received an urgent message describing the situation in

Halifax. A special relief train transporting doctors, nurses, and supplies was departing for the city from Wolfville, the next village over, at 12:00 p.m. Dr. Moore was requested to join them. Astounded by the news, the sixty-two-year-old physician quickly gathered all the instruments and supplies he had on hand and hurried down to the station.

A number of doctors and nurses had already boarded the train by the time Dr. Moore arrived. As he made his way down the aisle, Moore spied several familiar faces, including Dr. G. E. DeWitt and his daughter, Nellie. One face he didn't recognize, however, was that of Jerry Lonecloud. The sixty-three-year-old Mi'kmaq had been in Kentville on business when he got word of the disaster. Concerned about his family and community, Lonecloud had rushed to the station to catch the first train home.

At Windsor Junction, approximately a half-hour from Halifax, the relief train stopped to take on more medical supplies. The No. 10 train was idling on the tracks when they arrived. It had just come from Halifax and was en route to Truro with a load of casualties onboard. When the doctors and nurses spied the No. 10, they got their first hint of the extent of the catastrophe that awaited them down the line. With its shattered windows — several hastily boarded up to keep out the cold — the No. 10 looked as though it had just returned from the front lines.

For Major Avery DeWitt and Conductor Gillespie, meeting the trainload of doctors and nurses at Windsor Junction seemed like a godsend. They had far too many critically injured people aboard for one doctor to manage alone. Gillespie sent a dispatch to the relief train asking for volunteers to come aboard the No. 10 to assist with the casualties on the journey to Truro. One doctor and a nurse volunteered. Once they'd come aboard, both trains continued on their separate ways.

On the way to Truro, Major DeWitt worked at one end of the train, while the doctor and nurse from the relief train were

As days went by, more and more volunteers arrived to help in the search and relief efforts.

occupied at the opposite end. Many of the casualties had suffered serious eye injuries. Two critically injured patients in particular required immediate surgery to remove damaged eyeballs. Attempting to perform such delicate surgery aboard a moving train was a challenge. To make matters worse, the only surgical equipment DeWitt had to work with was forceps and a pair of scissors. But with the assistance of two passengers, DeWitt managed to perform both enucleations successfully. Any feeling of satisfaction the doctor may have derived from successfully completing the operations in such trying circumstances, however, was overshadowed by the fact that three children died before they reached Truro.

After a long, arduous trip, the No. 10 finally rolled into Truro at four that afternoon. As Major DeWitt was overseeing the unloading of his patients, he was astonished to see his father and sister, Nellie, at the other end of the platform. It turned out that they were the doctor and nurse that had been working at the opposite end of the train on the journey from Windsor Junction.

Since Truro had no hospital, the courthouse, academy, and fire hall had all been converted into temporary hospitals. However, all medical personnel in the area had already departed for Halifax, leaving only the DeWitts to care for the wounded. For the next week, they remained in Truro, working day and night without a thought for themselves.

* * *

When the train from Wolfville stopped at Windsor Junction to take on more supplies that morning, Jerry Lonecloud tried to hide his impatience. He had a terrible feeling of foreboding about what lay ahead and was anxious to get home. When Lonecloud saw the conductor making his way along the aisle, he stopped the man and asked how long it would be before they got moving.

"Not sure," the conductor muttered before hurrying off.

As time dragged on and the train showed no sign of getting underway, Lonecloud grew frantic. Finally, unable to sit still any longer, he decided to disembark and walk the rest of the way home.

* * *

It was only when Charles Duggan stepped off the ferry on Lower Water Street that he became aware of the fact that his clothes were still drenched as a result of being plunged into the harbour earlier. The temperature was dropping and Charles was freezing. As he passed McCartney's, he noticed that the windows had been shattered, but the billiard hall was still open. He decided to stop in to dry out his clothes and warm up a little before continuing northward.

When Charles finally reached North Street, a soldier stopped him from going any further. "This area has been cordoned off," the man said. "Only authorized personnel are allowed to enter."

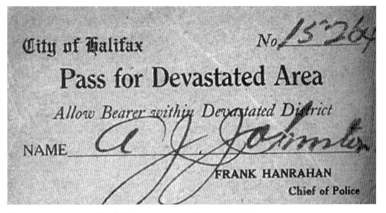

Passes were required for access to devastated areas.

"But my family is in there!" Charles said. "I've got to get home."

"Sorry son," the soldier replied. "If we let in everyone who had family in the area it would impede the search and rescue effort."

Charles stood there for a few minutes trying to decide what to do next. He felt numb and was having trouble thinking clearly. Finally, he decided to go to his sister's place on North Street. Surely she would have some news of the family.

When Charles arrived at his sister's he was relieved to find her house still standing. She, however, was in a terrible state. Charles felt as though he was sliding into a bottomless pit as she sat him down and told him that his wife Rita and son Warren, along with his mother, father, younger brother, and two sisters, were all dead. As he struggled to comprehend the horrific news, Charles recalled the heart-wrenching screams and cries for help he'd heard when he first regained consciousness on the Dartmouth shore. "Probably the cries I heard were the cries of my own people," he later told a reporter. He felt certain he'd never get those anguished cries out of his head.

Chapter 7
THE LIVING AND THE DEAD TOGETHER

When Florence Murray arrived at Camp Hill Hospital at 10:00 a.m., the place was in turmoil. The one hundred convalescent soldiers confined to the hospital had given up their beds and were busy cleaning up glass and plaster, boarding up windows, carrying in the wounded, and laying out mattresses to accommodate the flood of critically injured people pouring into the hospital. The first familiar face Florence saw was that of Dr. George MacIntosh, who was attending to a patient. She had begun assisting him when a military nurse came by. MacIntosh introduced Florence, explaining that she was a fourth-year medical student.

"Has your class had instruction in anaesthesia?" the nurse asked.

When Florence said they had, the nurse handed her a hypodermic outfit and a tube of morphine. "Go to the

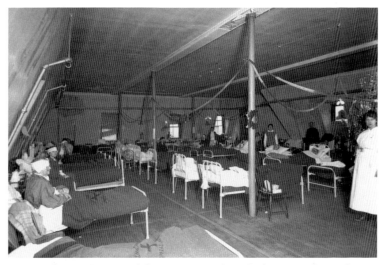

A typical scene in one of the temporary hospitals set up throughout the city.

operating room and give anaesthetics until this runs out," she said.

"But there are only fifteen tablets here," Florence pointed out.

"Don't worry," the nurse said. "An orderly has been sent out for more."

But after searching all over town, the orderly returned empty-handed. Florence tried to make the morphine go as far as possible, giving it only to "those making the most outcry."

The shortage of morphine meant that most patients, such as sixteen-year-old Alice MacDonald, suffered excruciating pain with no relief. A volunteer came across Alice lying on a mattress on the floor between two beds. The tall, dark-haired girl was an employee at Dominion Textiles Cotton Factory. The large factory employed about 300 people, most of whom were teenage girls and young women. The factory was hammered by the blast and many of the workers were crushed to death beneath heavy equipment when the floors collapsed. Others, pinned beneath beams and concrete, were burned alive by the raging inferno that consumed the remains of the building.

Alice had been working on the third floor that morning. When the fire broke out, she jumped out a window and landed on a pile of scrap iron, breaking both legs in several places. To make matters worse, a large piece of glass had been driven deep into her temple. The doctor who examined her felt she wouldn't survive her injuries. With nothing to ease the pain, Alice gnashed her teeth and writhed in agony all day and night while one of the convalescent soldiers crouched on the floor next to her, holding her hand.

Anaesthetics and painkillers weren't the only items in short supply that day. As Florence discovered, "There were unlimited supplies of bedding and mattresses, but nothing else that was needed." The operating room at Camp Hill hadn't yet been fitted up, which meant there wasn't any surgical equipment or operating tables in the hospital. "Doctors brought what they had themselves, but that was not much."

The Dominion Textiles factory before the explosion. Many workers did not survive the collapse of the building.

Temporary operating rooms were set up in the kitchen and dining room, where surgery was performed on kitchen tables. In some cases, kitchen utensils were used in lieu of surgical tools. And when surgical thread ran out, doctors resorted to using ordinary cotton thread to stitch up wounds.

The relief train from Wolfville carrying Dr. Willis Moore and his colleagues arrived on the outskirts of Richmond at about 3:30 p.m. The head of the medical committee, Lieutenant-Colonel Frederick McKelvey Bell, and Colonel Phinney were on hand to meet them. Since the crumpled tracks and mountains of debris prevented the train from going any further, the doctors and nurses were forced to walk about a kilometre before being met by a fleet of cars dispatched to take them to City Hall, where they would be detailed to a hospital.

As the doctors and nurses wound their way through the no man's land, they were shocked by what they encountered. They stumbled past mountains of debris containing cart wheels, broken furniture, clothing, dead horses, and mutilated corpses. Every so often, they came across piles of charred bodies "stacked like cordwood," awaiting delivery to the morgue. According to Dr. Moore, "No word except 'appalling' would indicate the horrors of the scene."

The scenes in the hospital were almost as bad. At the entrance to Camp Hill Hospital, a steady stream of vehicles dropped off load after load of casualties. And the stretcher-bearers never ceased carrying people in. Dr. Moore was astonished to find that men, women, and children were "literally packed into the wards like sardines." By that time, 1,400 critically injured people were crammed into a space designed to hold fewer than 250. Every square inch of space throughout the hospital was utilized, including the corridors, offices, and storage rooms. Mattresses lined the floors, and everyone had to step carefully to avoid tripping over the multitude of filthy, blood-soaked patients, many of whom were so badly mangled that it was difficult to discern age or sex. One Sister of Charity described the victims as "shapeless masses of

Children gathered in a temporary hospital after the explosion.

gore." Many were bathed in blood; others were soaked from the tidal wave or from being plunged into the harbour. With the windows out and the doors constantly opening as more patients were brought in, the corridors were freezing cold. As a result, those in wet clothing suffered terribly and many died of exposure. In one storage room, Florence Murray came upon a woman cradling her baby girl in her arms. The pair were drenched and had been left without attention all day. Sadly, the baby died of exposure.

Adding to the turmoil was the fact that throughout the day, hordes of people wandered through the wards, desperately searching for missing loved ones. In the chaos following the blast, hundreds of children became separated from their parents, many never to be reunited.

After being shown to a makeshift operating room, Dr. Moore began the onerous task of trying to mend the endless stream of battered and broken bodies. The variety and severity of wounds, he noted, were extraordinary. Third degree

A typical surgical kit, which would have been used by many doctors at that time.

burns, fractures of all kinds, amputated limbs, gashes, facial lacerations, and eye injuries were widespread. Flying glass and shrapnel left many horribly disfigured. One woman's face was sliced almost completely off. It hung by a small flap of skin, "like a trap-door...the nasal and frontal bones were cut away and the base of the brain was exposed." In most cases, the wounds were packed with dirt, plaster, cinders, and glass, making the task of patching them up that much more difficult.

The poor lighting and lack of proper equipment and supplies only made the doctor's job more difficult. After several hours of operating non-stop, Dr. Moore was exhausted and his nerves were frayed. When a volunteer accidentally knocked over a tray of surgical instruments, Moore snapped at her. Seeing the look of dismay on the young woman's face, he quickly apologized, helped her pick up the instruments, and got back to work.

* * *

Over at the Victoria General, Fred Longland reported to the front desk and said he'd been summoned about an unidentified man in a coma who had been calling out his name. When the nurse showed Fred to the man's bedside, he was more puzzled than ever.

"Do you recognize him?" the nurse asked.

Fred shook his head. The patient appeared to be terribly jaundiced and was "pitted all over with what looked like bits of cinder." Oddly, the only words the mysterious person had spoken since being admitted were "Fred Longland." Since he had only arrived in the city that day, and didn't know anyone there, Fred was stumped. He asked the staff to contact him if there was any change in the patient's condition and returned to the *Niobe*.

It was three weeks before the unidentified man came out of his coma and Fred was contacted again. When he arrived at the patient's bedside this time, he was surprised to see the man sitting up and looking quite normal. As it turned out, he was one of Fred's childhood friends from Waterloo, Ontario.

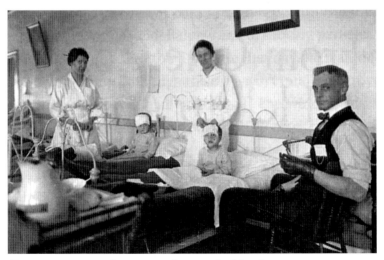

Doctor, nurses, and young patients at St. Mary's.

Astonishingly, the man had remembered hearing that Fred Longland had been posted to Halifax. And in his comatose state, this was the only name he had spoken.

* * *

As Evelyn Fox and her friends stood around the fire in the field off St. Margaret's Bay Road that afternoon, a young woman with a baby in her arms came along. The woman looked exhausted. Her dress was tattered and grimy, and her face was smeared with soot. When the girls offered to hold the baby while she rested by the fire, the woman gratefully handed it over, saying, "I just can't carry the poor little thing any farther."

"What's its name?" asked Hazel.

"I haven't any idea," the woman replied.

Seeing the look of astonishment on the girls' faces, she explained how the baby had come to be in her possession. "My house fell on me," she said. "I don't know how I managed to get out. All around, people were running or trapped and screaming in the fires. I ran. Someone put this baby in my arms; I kept running."

The baby wasn't wearing a hat or coat, and Evelyn noticed that its elaborately embroidered gown was bloodstained. Who were its parents? Were they frantically searching through smoking rubble for their child at that very moment? Or had they perished in the explosion?

After resting for a few minutes, the young woman rose to leave. When Hazel went to hand the baby over to her, she put her hands up and backed away. "I haven't anyone to turn to and nowhere to go," she said in a weary monotone. "The baby will be better off with you girls." Dumbfounded, the girls simply stood and stared as the woman turned and tramped across the field.

Hungry and in need of changing, the infant howled constantly. The girls took turns trying to pacify it, pacing back and forth and rocking it while making cooing sounds. When Evelyn's turn came, she wrapped her coat around it and held it close, hoping that would help. But the baby continued to howl, its tiny body tensing up with each ragged scream.

After what seemed like hours, a young woman on a cart pulled up. On the back of the cart were a few meagre belongings and several children. The oddly dressed woman jumped down and shuffled over to the fire. A pair of men's rubber boots flopped on her feet, and a large man's overcoat hung loosely from her narrow shoulders.

"I heard a baby crying," she said. The girls eagerly revealed the baby, explaining how they'd acquired it.

"It won't stop crying," they wailed.

The woman took a look at the child. "It's hungry," she said matter-of-factly. "I'd better take it. I have relatives ten miles farther on, and if I can get that far, they'll have milk."

Relieved to be free of the responsibility, the teenagers didn't think twice before handing the baby over. The woman tucked it beneath the bulky overcoat, climbed back onto the cart, gave the reins a snap, and the nag plodded off.

Exhausted from the effort of trying to comfort the infant, Evelyn suddenly felt cold, hungry, and miles from home. She thought of her father. Was he out there somewhere, searching for her? She decided it was time to start making her way home. She invited Laurence to come home with her, but he refused, saying he'd be fine outdoors. But Evelyn wouldn't hear of it.

"I have a brother in France," she said. "If our house is still standing, there'll be room in it for a returned soldier."

As they set out along the railway tracks heading for Fairview, the clear blue skies turned grey. By the time they reached Rockingham — six kilometres past the devastated North End — dusk was closing in. The girls were relieved when they spied the glowing taillights of a train idling on the tracks.

When they climbed aboard, Evelyn noticed that rather

A view of the city, looking inland from the waterfront.

than being filled with the usual commuters heading home to the suburbs after a day at work, the cars were packed with bloodied, bandaged individuals whose faces appeared "emptied and dulled by shock and grief." Since city hospitals and shelters were all filled to capacity, any victims who were able to make the trip were being transported elsewhere. This trainload was on its way to Truro, where shelters and temporary hospitals had been set up to house the survivors.

Bedford was immersed in darkness by the time Evelyn and her friends arrived. The girls said their goodbyes at the station and went their separate ways. As Evelyn stumbled through the gloom, Laurence limped along behind her. Now that she was almost home, she began to worry about what awaited her there and whether or not her parents would approve of her dragging a complete stranger home.

The house was cloaked in darkness by the time they arrived. From the outside, it was impossible to tell if anyone was home or not. Evelyn took a deep breath and pushed the door open. As they stepped in out of the cold, she was relieved to find her whole family waiting for her. She nervously introduced Laurence, explaining that he had given up his bed at Camp Hill Hospital and had nowhere to sleep that night. There was a brief pause before Mr. Fox shook the soldier's hand. "Glad to meet you, son," he said. "Let me take your coat."

* * *

The sun was low in the afternoon sky when a rescue party from the *Highflyer* happened upon the captain and crew of the *Mont-Blanc.* Captain Le Médec and his men had been wandering around Dartmouth for hours in search of a doctor to attend to their critically injured crewmember. The men were disoriented and appalled by the sights they'd witnessed that afternoon. But at that point, they weren't yet aware of the full extent of the disaster. The commanding officer of the rescue party ordered his men to take Le Médec and his crew back to the *Highflyer,* where they would be held pending an investigation into the explosion.

* * *

As Ralph Proctor slid behind the wheel of the Model T and started it up, he prayed she would make it up Cogswell and over to Camp Hill one more time. He'd already made more than a dozen trips to and from the hospital that day, and both he and the car were feeling the effects. The tires — slashed by glass and shrapnel — were in tatters. Worse, the wound in his lung had reopened, and his back was killing him. He'd had one passenger — a man who had been crushed by a toppling house — die before they reached their destination. And not long after that, Ralph and his passengers had narrowly escaped with their lives when the front of a blazing two-story house toppled into the street just as they were abreast of it. As the fiery beams crashed down on the car, shattering the

The fire truck Patricia, *pictured after sustaining damage during the explosion.*

windshield, Ralph gasped, sucking particles of glass into his lungs. For the first time that day, he feared for his own well-being. Although the car wasn't totally destroyed in the incident, it was badly damaged. The windshield was gone, the mud guard crumpled, and the cowl smashed in. Nevertheless, he soldiered on, driven perhaps by the memory of lying wounded in the frozen muck of no man's land at Vimy.

Chapter 8
FROM ONE CORNER OF HELL TO ANOTHER

By mid-afternoon, word of the disaster had spread throughout the region and down the eastern seaboard. Moncton, Truro, New Glasgow, and Boston all scrambled to organize relief trains to carry medical personnel and supplies to the beleaguered city as soon as possible. The train from New Glasgow, a small town about 165 kilometres north of Halifax, departed at noon. Onboard were eleven doctors, including George Cox, a forty-six-year-old ophthalmologist. Cox had been in the neighbouring village of Stellarton, performing an operation, when he heard about the explosion and the relief train. Afterwards, he rushed home and rounded up whatever supplies he had on hand before heading down to the station. He arrived just as group of local firemen finished loading a fire engine and several hundred metres of hose on board.

By the time the train rolled to a halt on the outskirts of Richmond at 5:30 p.m. that evening, darkness was descending.

Since there were no cars to meet them, the doctors and nurses were forced to pick their way through the ruins on foot, following the same route taken by Dr. Moore and the others earlier that afternoon. As he stumbled over debris and passed piles of twisted, blackened corpses, Cox felt as though he was "going from one corner of Hell to another."

When he arrived at Camp Hill Hospital, the matron set him up in a corner of a dimly lit room. At first, Cox pitched in by working on all types of wounds. But after a few hours, he realized that his experience as an ocular surgeon could be put to far greater use, and he set out through the teeming wards and gloomy corridors in search of eye injuries. He didn't have to look far. Before long, he had rounded up enough eye work to keep him busy for several days. The injuries included eyelids that were "cut into literal fringes" and eyeballs that appeared to be nothing but "bags of glass." Cox observed that in some cases, "there were no more eyeballs. It was as if the ball had been laid open and then stuffed with pieces of glass or sometimes crockery, brick splinters." Many doctors wouldn't have bothered to try to save the eye in such cases, but Cox was determined to save the sight of as many of these unfortunate individuals as possible.

Although several other doctors were also performing eye surgery, for the next five days Dr. Cox did nothing but repair eyes, only stopping to rest when he was too exhausted to stay on his feet another moment. In total, Cox performed seventy-five enucleations. In four or five cases, he was forced to remove both eyeballs.

* * *

As the afternoon wore on, it became increasingly clear to Dr. Almon that Rockhead Hospital was uninhabitable. The roof was all but gone, there was no heat, and the floors were flooded. Worried that under these circumstances many patients would not survive the night, the doctor began making arrangements

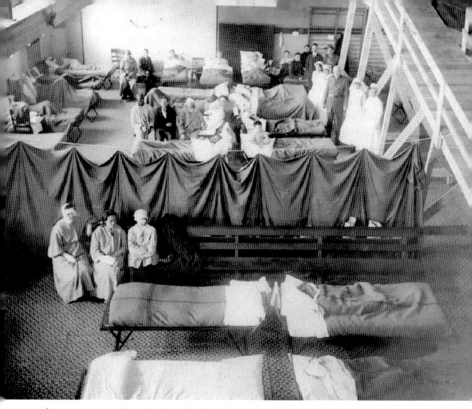

The temporary hospital at the YMCA.

to decamp. It was early evening by the time he'd finalized the plan to transport the patients from Rockhead to other medical facilities in the area. By then, the USS *Old Colony*, the YMCA, and Saint Mary's College, among others, had been converted into temporary hospitals, bringing the total number of medical facilities in operation to sixteen.

Catherine James was among those transferred to Camp Hill Hospital that night. She would remain there for a week before she was well enough to move to a shelter. On December 10, her brother-in-law, Robert, arrived from Mahone Bay and began searching for Jack. After two days of combing the city, Robert finally located his brother's body in the temporary morgue. With her husband dead, Catherine was left penniless, homeless, and almost entirely alone in the world.

* * *

At Camp Hill Hospital, Florence Murray surveyed the jumbled mass of humanity crowding the ward. She had been dressing wounds, administering morphine, picking glass out of people, and offering whatever aid or comfort she could all day. There seemed to be no end to the stream of wounded and dying pouring in. And the more patients that arrived, the more chaotic things became. Hundreds of anxious people straggled through the wards, seeking missing family members. What's more, the matron had caught several individuals sneaking into the hospital and stealing food as well as items that belonged to the dead and dying. She had also discovered several young girls in the wards, whom she felt had come in out of curiosity and stayed to chat up the convalescent soldiers. The matron had warned Florence to keep an eye out for these interlopers, but she had far more important things to worry about than a few silly young girls. She'd received word earlier that her aunt and uncle's house on Veith Street had been destroyed in the blast. Her aunt was missing and was believed to be entombed beneath the ruins of her house. Although the news was distressing, Florence remained on duty. At the moment, she felt it was more important to focus on the living. There would be time to mourn the dead once the crisis had passed.

* * *

After he'd walked for hours, Jerry Lonecloud finally arrived back at Turtle Grove at dusk. As he approached the Mi'kmaq settlement, his worst fears were confirmed. Turtle Grove had taken the full force of the blast. When J. H. Mitchell of the Halifax Disaster Record Office visited the settlement some days later, he described the devastation as "incomprehensible." Nothing, not even the pines that used to shade the houses, remained standing. "Everything is gone," Mitchell wrote. "Of some houses there is absolutely no vestige, not even of ashes… Clothing, furniture, stoves, trunks, etc., are everywhere." Nine of the twenty-one residents of Turtle Grove died in the explosion;

The Mi'kmaq school in Turtle Grove was destroyed in the explosion.

the rest were seriously wounded. Among those killed were Jerry Lonecloud's daughters, Rosie and Hannah. The loss of his two beloved daughters, as well as his home and half the community, was a devastating blow for the Mi'kmaq elder.

* * *

City Hall had been a hive of activity all afternoon as an army of volunteers organized food distribution, medical care, and shelter. The temperature had been dropping steadily all afternoon, and it was vital that shelters be prepared to take in as many as possible that night. This meant cots, bedding, and other essential items had to be rounded up, partitions erected, windows boarded up, and washroom facilities improvised.

By early evening, several shelters opened their doors and people began pouring in, grateful to have someplace to lay their head that night. In addition to the public shelters, dozens of private citizens whose homes hadn't been damaged took in as many refugees as they could manage. But in spite

Morgues quickly filled with bodies, waiting to be identified.

of these efforts, many people were still forced to spend the night on the streets, huddling in doorways, railway cars, and abandoned buildings.

That night, Ada Moore curled up on the floor of an empty house in Rockingham, where she and the others had ended up after fleeing the city. The next day, Ada would make her way to her married daughter's place on Willow Street. There, she would finally learn the fate of her husband Charles and her four missing children. Fortunately, the children had survived, although they were injured and in hospital. But Charles was killed in the blast.

In addition to losing her husband and four youngest children in the disaster, Ada also lost two sisters, four brothers, her mother, three sisters-in-law, and twenty-five nieces and nephews.

* * *

While arrangements were being made to house and feed the survivors, a detail of soldiers had been busy getting the temporary mortuary in the Chebucto Road School up and running. In order to make the building habitable, the windows had to be boarded up and electric lights and stoves installed. Once these details were taken care of, the men realized they needed water for washing the bodies. Since the school had no running water, it had to be carried in from nearby homes. With these preparations complete, the men began the heart-wrenching task of carrying in the bodies and preparing them to be identified by family members.

At 6:00 p.m. the mortuary opened its doors to the public. By that time, a long line of desperate people was waiting outside. Most had spent the day wandering through hospital wards and private funeral parlours searching for missing loved ones. They were dirty, dazed, and exhausted. While they waited, men hunched their shoulders against the cold, smoked, and stared grimly into the distance. A few women sobbed quietly, while others spoke in whispers to their neighbours, sharing information about shelters and food depots.

Like most others, Chris Coleman had come here as a last resort. He'd spent the afternoon going from one hospital to another in search of his younger brother, Vincent. When he came across his sister-in-law, Frances, at Camp Hill earlier, Chris had barely recognized her. Frances had always taken pride in her appearance, but that afternoon her luxuriant hair, normally neatly swept up in a chignon, hung in limp strands around her face, and her dress was torn and dirty.

Chris could still remember the day Vincent had first brought Frances home to introduce her to the family. He'd never seen his brother so crazy about a woman before. And even after fifteen years of marriage, it was clear that the couple were still very much in love. Before leaving the hospital, Chris had promised to return as soon as he had any news about Vincent.

When his turn came to enter the morgue, Chris was filled with dread. He reluctantly followed the soldier down into the dank basement, where row upon row of inert, white-sheeted mounds were laid out beneath the glare of bare bulbs.

* * *

Captain Horatio Brannen's wife, Susie, had already been informed of her husband's death by the time her son Walter arrived home that evening. The youth was in a deep state of shock, and looked like "a blackened, powder-stained ghost of a man." Everything but his underwear had been ripped off in the explosion. And at some point during the day, someone had taken pity on him and wrapped a red tablecloth around his shoulders to keep him from freezing. It was a miracle that he and William Knickerson had survived the explosion with only superficial wounds. These physical wounds would heal eventually; the emotional scars, however, would be with them forever.

* * *

Fires still blazed throughout Richmond as rescue workers continued to comb the ruins for survivors. By 11:00 p.m., Ralph Proctor's back and leg were killing him. He'd been driving through the ruins non-stop since morning. As he dropped off his last load of casualties at Camp Hill, one of the stretcher-bearers he'd spoken to a few times that day asked, "How many is that now, soldier?"

Ralph did a quick tally. "About twenty-three trips, I think."

"Time to knock off for a few hours," the stretcher-bearer said. "Otherwise we'll end up carrying your sorry behind in next."

* * *

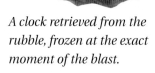

A clock retrieved from the rubble, frozen at the exact moment of the blast.

The moment Frances Coleman saw Chris picking his way across

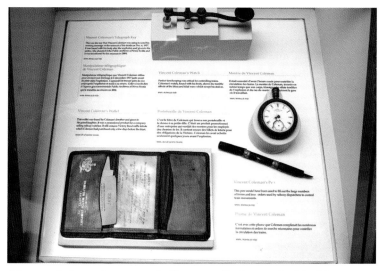

Vincent Coleman's personal effects, on display at the Maritime Museum of the Atlantic, including his watch and the remains of his telegraph key.

the crowded ward that evening, she knew the news was bad. Her brother-in-law's face was drawn and pale, and the usual twinkle in his eye had been extinguished. He looked as though he'd aged ten years since that afternoon. She tried to maintain her composure as he took her hand, saying, "I'm so sorry, Frances…"

Vincent had died at his post, tapping out a warning to incoming trains to stay clear. His co-worker, William Lovett, had lived long enough to tell the story of how the dispatcher had heroically sacrificed his own life in an effort to save hundreds of others. Vincent's body had been burned beyond recognition. The only means of identification were the watch and wallet found on the remains.

Frances, who was just forty years old, had already lost her father, a son, and now her husband — more loss than most people experience in a lifetime. After Chris left, she tried to shut out all the horror surrounding her and go to sleep. But thoughts of Vincent, her children, and the tragic events of the

Soldiers in thick winter uniforms braved heavy snowfall to continue search and rescue efforts.

day kept churning through her mind. Would the pain and sorrow of this day never end?

* * *

As the night wore on, temperatures plunged until it was bitterly cold and winds picked up as the first few flurries of what would be the worst blizzard to hit Halifax in years began to fall. Those whose houses were still standing huddled by fires as snow gusted in around hastily boarded up windows and doors. In the harbour, the icy winds lashed battered ships and turned the port into "a wild sea." Crews cursed the cold as they worked to secure the unmoored vessels drifting helplessly on the currents. It was as though a supernatural power had unleashed a wrath of biblical proportions upon the stricken city.

EPILOGUE

The next day, the *Morning Chronicle*'s bold black headline declared:

HALIFAX IN RUINS

Collision which occurred at 9:05 yesterday morning has laid the Northern End of the city in ruins. Mont-Blanc a French munitions boat collides in the harbour with a Belgian relief ship and blows up. — Dead number hundreds and casualties are known to be in the thousands. — Every available place in the city being utilized as emergency morgues and hospitals. — No cause yet found for the collision. — Crowds of frenzied people rush through streets fleeing from what was first thought to be a German raid. — Streets littered with dead. — Practically two square miles of territory a burning ruin.

Next to the story, long columns listed the missing and those known (or thought to be) dead. In fact, approximately 2,000 people died as a result of the explosion. Another 9,000 were injured. Of those who did survive, 20,000 found themselves homeless,

The Halifax Explosion monument.

destitute, and facing a grim winter as they tried to rebuild their shattered lives.

Eight days after the blast, the temporary morgue in the Chebucto Road School still held 350 unidentified bodies, soldiers were still digging bodies from the ruins, and family members were still desperately searching for missing loved ones. Dozens of infants and young children were orphaned. Day after day, the newspapers were filled with postings describing children found, and others seeking missing persons.

The number of people blinded in the explosion was staggering. It is estimated that between 200 and 600 lost their vision when windows across the city shattered in the blast. In the days following the explosion, hundreds of operations were performed to remove hopelessly damaged eyes. At the Victoria General Hospital alone, at least sixty enucleations were reported in a single day.

The explosion left many survivors both physically and psychologically scarred for life. Months after the blast, deep psychological effects were only beginning to surface. Many victims suffered complete nervous and mental collapse. Some, unable to come to terms with the horror and trauma they had experienced, committed suicide. Others lived in constant dread of another explosion. Loud noises or fire often triggered a panic response among the survivors.

* * *

When word of the explosion spread, aid began pouring in from all over the world. The American response in particular was overwhelmingly generous. Relief trains from Boston and New York carrying food, medical supplies and equipment, and hospital staff were organized and dispatched within hours of the blast. Many more relief trains followed. A Massachusetts-Halifax Relief Committee was established, and the outpouring of generosity from the people of that state was remarkable. The relief committee sent shiploads of

Relief workers and volunteers, photographed disembarking from a relief train.

glass, lumber, building supplies, clothing, blankets, food, and new trucks. Furthermore, a battalion of Massachusetts trade workers, including carpenters, engineers, construction workers, glaziers, and plumbers, arrived to help rebuild the city. While a plea for doctors and nurses brought hundreds from the East Coast to Halifax, including an entire medical team from Harvard University.

In addition to the outpouring of generosity from countries, states, and provinces, benevolent individuals and corporations also provided assistance. Sir John Eaton, president of T. Eaton Co., donated millions of dollars worth of medical supplies and equipment, clothing, building materials, and household goods. Not only did Eaton donate these goods, he delivered them in person and oversaw their distribution.

Shortly after the disaster, Haligonians began seeking answers and demanding justice. Who was to blame? How would they be punished for their crime? For those whose homes and families had been wiped out, the need for justice was great. An inquiry into the cause of the explosion began on December 13, 1917. Captain Aimé Le Médec was the first witness to take the stand.

In all, more than twenty witnesses testified, including crewmembers of the *Imo* and the *Mont-Blanc.* Proceedings came to an end on January 28, 1918. On February 4, Justice Drysdale released the findings. Since Captain Hakkon From and William Hayes were both dead, blame was placed squarely on the shoulders of the captain and pilot of the *Mont-Blanc* and Commander Frederick Wyatt, the Chief Examining Officer for the Port of Halifax. Wyatt was implicated, as he had been responsible for all movements of large vessels in the harbour.

Once Justice Drysdale's findings were released, Wyatt, Le Médec, and Francis Mackey were all placed under arrest and charged with manslaughter. Eventually, however, all charges were dropped. Aimé Le Médec continued serving as captain with the Compagnie Générale Transatlantique for another

A view of the crowds gathered in Halifax for the mass funeral service held to honour the 200 unidentified dead.

four years. On his retirement from the merchant marine, Le Médec was awarded the Chevalier de la Légion d'Honneur. Francis Mackey, whose pilot's licence had been revoked during the proceedings, had his licence reinstated. He continued working as a harbour pilot. And Commander Wyatt was quietly shuffled off to another location.

Anti-German sentiment, rampant before the explosion, reached a fevered pitch during the inquiry. In the minds of many, there was no doubt that the enemy was to blame for the catastrophe. Enemy spies plotting sabotage were believed to be everywhere. A vicious campaign flared up against anyone of German descent. Angry mobs attacked innocent Germans in the streets and vandalized their homes. Finally, all Germans living in the city were rounded up and placed under arrest.

The healing process began on December 17 with a mass, multi-denominational funeral service for the 200 unidentified dead remaining in the morgue. Thousands crowded in and around the Chebucto Road School yard to watch the moving service. While the mourners sang hymns, soldiers carried out the coffins and laid them out one by one.

BIBLIOGRAPHY

Armstrong, John Griffith. *The Halifax Explosion and the Royal Canadian Navy: Inquiry and Intrigue.* Vancouver: UBC Press, 2002.

Bird, Michael J. *The Town that Died: The True Story of the Greatest Man-Made Explosion Before Hiroshima.* Toronto: McGraw-Hill Ryerson Ltd., 1962.

Boileau, John. *Halifax & the Royal Canadian Navy.* Halifax: Nimbus Publishing, 2010.

Chapman, Harry. *Dartmouth's Day of Anguish.* Dartmouth: The Dartmouth Historical Society, 1992.

Flemming, David B. *Explosion in Halifax Harbour: The Illustrated Account of a Disaster That Shook the World.* Halifax: Formac Publishing, 2004.

Kitz, Janet F. *Shattered City: The Halifax Explosion and the Road to Recovery.* Halifax: Nimbus Publishing, 1989.

MacDonald, Laura M. *Curse of the Narrows: The Halifax Disaster of 1917.* Toronto: HarperCollins Publishers, 2005.

Metson, Graham, ed. *The Halifax Explosion: December 6, 1917.* Toronto: McGraw-Hill Ryerson Ltd., 1978.

Murray, Florence J. *At the Foot of Dragon Hill.* New York: Dutton, 1975.

Raddall, Thomas H. *Halifax: Warden of the North.* Halifax: Nimbus, 1993.

Richardson, Evelyn M. "The Halifax Explosion — 1917." *The Nova Scotia Historical Quarterly* 7, no. 4 (1977): 305–330.

Ruffman, Alan and Colin D. Howell, eds. *Ground Zero: A Reassessment of the 1917 Explosion in Halifax Harbour.* Halifax: Nimbus Publishing and the Gorsebrook Research Institute, 1994.

Smith, S. K. *Heart Throbs of the Halifax Horror.* Halifax: Gerald E. Weir, 1918.

ACKNOWLEDGEMENTS

I'm eternally grateful that Archibald MacMechan and his staff at the Halifax Disaster Record Office had the foresight to collect hundreds of personal narratives from the survivors in the weeks and months following the explosion. These narratives, as well as the letters, journals, news clippings and reports held in the Nova Scotia Archives and Record Management are the primary sources on which I drew to piece together this account. In addition, the NSARM online Explosion Remembrance Book proved to be an invaluable source of information. Evelyn M. Richardson's detailed firsthand account, "The Halifax Explosion — 1917" provided a glimpse of the disaster through the eyes of a teenager. And the unpublished manuscripts of G. K. Brannen and Thelma Dasbourg on Captain Horatio Brannen in the Maritime Museum of the Atlantic offered insights into the life of this admirable figure.

I am deeply indebted to a number of people who helped make this book a reality. Heartfelt thanks to Janette Snooks and Anne Finlayson for the use of the photographs and for graciously sharing memories information about their parents and grandparents, Vincent and Frances Coleman; and to Paula Fenwick and her son, Greg Fenwick, for providing information about Paula's father, Ralph Proctor. Thanks also to Alan Ruffman for his suggestions; Jim Simpson for the tour of the explosion sites; Dan Conlin, Curator of Maritime History at the Maritime Museum of the Atlantic, for his helpful advice and assistance; and the wonderful staff at the Nova Scotia Archives and Record Management for all their help. Many thanks also to Nancy Sewell at Formac Publishing and to Jerry Lockett for his meticulous copy editing. Finally, this book would not have been possible without the understanding, support, and encouragement of my husband, Doug.

Photo Credits

Alan Ruffman Collection: 38

An Illustrated Collection of Tugboats to Remember, Austin Dwyer: 20

City of Toronto Archives: front cover, 52, 63, 68, 78, 84, 86, 98, 101, 103, 123

Curse of the Narrows: 76, 94

David B. Flemming: 5, 14

DiAnn L'Roy: 54

Formac Publishing Company Ltd.: 43 (left), 66, 91, 120

Gary Castle Photography: 34

Janet Maybee, author of *Aftershock: The Halifax Explosion and Persecution of Pilot Francis Mackey*: 12, 42

Jewish Heritage Center at the New England Historic Genealogical Society, Boston, Massachusetts: back cover, 69

Library and Archives Canada: back cover, 29, 73, 118

Maritime Museum of the Atlantic: back cover, 8, 9, 11, 15, 21, 24, 26, 30, 35, 36, 37, 43 (bottom), 49, 81, 92, 106, 108, 117

Naval Historical Center: 89

Nova Scotia Archives: back cover, 16, 17, 19, 25, 31, 33, 40, 41, 44, 45, 46, 47, 51, 56, 57, 58, 60, 65, 74, 77, 82, 83, 85, 91, 96, 99, 111, 113, 114, 121

Nova Scotia Museum: 28

Proctor Family Collection: 72

Warren Anatomical Museum: 102

Wikipedia: 10, 23, 61, 116

INDEX

Photographic references appear in italics.